To Scipione.
We invented this together,
our 'garden that wasn't',
and together we will walk through it every day,
smiling and holding hands.

16 - 10 - 2002

Miki Borghese

Le Case del Biviere

The garden that wasn't

SilvanaEditoriale

Watercolours by Enza Signorelli

Silvana Editoriale

Projects and realisation
Arti Grafiche Amilcare Pizzi Spa

Direction
Dario Cimorelli

Editor
Anna Albano

Editing
Margherita Guerritore

Layout
Pierluigi Giussani

To get to the garden of Case del Biviere, you must cross a spoiled and often oftentimes foul-smelling terrain that visitors find baffling. The agricultural environment has been completely neglected, the roads and low walls are covered with weeds, and from the narrow bridge that crosses the Lentini you can see the riverbanks overrun with garbage. Scraggly flocks of sheep invade the remains of an abandoned farming town whose charming architecture deserves being restored.
'Where am I being taken?' is the visitor's unspoken question. You come to a wall with a long cascade of purple bougainvillea, and to a pale stone portal edged in grey lava stone.
The immense dark-green gate swings open... and you're taken by surprise, for you are entering 'the garden of legend'. Scipione, the master of the house, left us on 21 July 2001. Everything came to a standstill, motionless. The garden – our garden – held its breath with Monica, Sofia, Maria della Neve and Giangiacomo. But Scipione returns with the faint glimmer of dawn, with the dazzling noon, with the midday breeze. And it is here, among the multiform shapes of these succulents, amidst the colours of the jacarandas, the bougainvillea, the *Parkinsonia*, the *Solandra*, the *Corysia*, the oleanders, the leadworts, and accompanied by the scent of citrus blossoms, roses, fragrant herbs and jasmine, that we find him again, day after day.

Miki Borghese

Foreword

This enchanting book is an inspiring record of a most remarkable garden, island, husband and wife. Its kind, shrewd eye for Sicily and its landscape leads on to a modest account of the making of a heavenly garden in the most unpromising circumstances. Even now, the view beyond Case del Biviere is brown and bleak, more than enough for most of us in the dark months of the year. When the Borgheses returned to live here in the sixties, it was as awkward and unlikely a setting for a fine garden as you could imagine. It is now transformed and is a witness to their years of quiet devotion and determined taste. 'The only thing to do was to avoid getting depressed, consider myself a pioneer, roll up my sleeves and try to turn an uninhabitable spot into a place to live' (p. 28). Thirty years later, when I first saw it, the 'uninhabitable spot' had become the most sensitive and thoughtfully planted garden in the great heat of the South. This book gives us several clues as to how this result has come about. The charming idea of short 'biographies' to each plant reminds us of the makers' constant vigilance, all over Sicily and elsewhere, for handsome, and often rare, 'architectural' plants to give the garden strong lines. The sketches of Sicilian life at the beginning of the book can hardly conceal their author's spirit, observation and imagination. These qualities cannot be bought in a garden centre or from a ready-made design. The Biviere garden combines spiky, cactus-like focal points with flowers galore in an imaginative informality: roses, even, where there was once the mooring for boats on Hercules the hero's mythical lake. It is truly cosmopolitan while remaining individual, here something seen in South Africa, there a tree from Morocco and everywhere the unusual plants which have been bought in Sicily itself. It is the only fine garden which I know on the site of a former harbour. It is the best private garden made in Sicily or Italy in the past forty years. Readers of its maker's memories and sharp-eyed notes will begin to understand why.

Robin Lane Fox

Scipione and Miki with the grapefruits of the terrace.

The garden that wasn't

Introduction

According to legend, Hercules, the son of Jupiter, decided to give Ceres, goddess of the harvest, the pelt of the invulnerable Nemean lion he had slain. When he arrived in the city of the Lestrigons where the goddess lived, he made a lake spring forth on the spot and it was named after him: Lacuus Erculeus. To hand down the story of his undertaking, the nearby city was thus named 'Leontio'.

Over the centuries, the name of the lake and the outlying districts was changed to 'Biviere', derived from the Arab 'Veverè', which meant drinking trough for flocks or fish hatchery. If you look closely at the countryside, you can find the remains of the *morti*, real chambers carved in the tuff where the fish, carried by the current through long manmade channels, would be trapped, making them easier to catch.

Preserved at the State Archives of Palermo is the original document of the Edict of King Martin who, in 1392, granted the fief of 'Il Biviere di Lentini' to a maternal ancestor of Scipione Borghese. From 1393 through today, the fief has undergone various transformations, including the reclamation work started in 1930, until it finally became the home of Scipione and Maria Carla Borghese thirty years ago.

A love and passion for plants has transformed what was once a desolate place, surrounded only by stones and dust, into a

unique and particular Mediterranean garden. The dusty rocks have made room for the fertile soil trapped by the waters of the lake for thousands of years. Memories of the past have taken on a different shape: they are no longer unfeeling but are tied irrevocably to their surroundings. The ancient port facing south, enclosed by enormous boulders hewn by hand, is now the charming and luxuriant welcome to the main façade of Case del Biviere. On the jetties, restored with loving attention and grace, an extraordinary collection of succulents brought in from many far-off countries forms what looks like a walkway of green statues.
The visitor steps into a harmonious place that is coloured with orange and jasmine, and that reflects the wise inspiration of those who have loved this land for centuries.
If time has ever found a reason to flow, then amidst these fragrances and colours it will find a reason to stand still, to allow you to enjoy all its intense beauty and tranquillity. And we too await you here, to give you the joy of discovering such a unique place, suspended between reality and history – as if, once again, the goddess Ceres had decided to make Case del Biviere her divine abode.

Arrival in Sicily

According to a Chinese proverb, 'Life begins the day you start a garden'.
It was 1967 and I was 37 years old when the idea came to me to create a garden in that desolate place. Until then, I had never had either the opportunity or the occasion to think about a garden, and my knowledge of flowers and botany was scanty and superficial. I loved nature – its colours, its smells, its silences and its message – but the city also fascinated me with its wealth of treasures waiting to be discovered, its memories and its history.

Before I begin the story of how my beloved garden came to be, I must tell you about a several episodes in my Sicilian life, to give you a better idea of my profound ties to this land and the passion that, little by little and almost without my even realising it, took over my soul and sparked my imagination to shape the untilled land around Case del Biviere and give it meaning.
It was February of 1957. In Rome, it was drizzly and cold, one of those sad, grey, winter days when the light of spring is still far away. After we had been airborne for about two hours, the captain announced that we were about to fly over the Aeolian Islands and that we would be landing in Catania shortly. It was my first trip to Sicily and, seen from above, the Lipari Islands seemed to float on that unmoving blue water.
A short time later, snow-covered Etna appeared to our left, with a big plume of smoke crowning the central crater. It was a marvellous view that gave me an inkling of all the sensations I was about to experience.
Scipione was there to meet me, and we happily left for Siracusa by car. The road wasn't the same as it is now: you had to take the Catania-Lentini-Siracusa, as winding and varied as all the Sicilian roads were back then.
We were supposed to stop in Biviere to meet the squire Zuccalà, who was the overseer for the area.
I didn't find the place particularly attractive. I remember cows in a pen, and some sad and rundown old houses without any greenery around them. It was not the destination of our trip and I had no premonition about it.
Siracusa enchanted me with its sapphire sea, the bougainvillea of Villa Politi in every possible shade of red and purple, the white stone of Ortigia, the papyruses of Fonte Aretusa, and the lone

Venus in that little hall reserved just for her in the archaeological museum of Piazza Duomo. It was heaven on earth, a land blessed by the gods who still lived there and were as vivid and tangibly present as they are at the Acropolis in Athens or at dawn on the beach of Monemvassia along the Peloponnesian coast.
I realised that from then on, the island of Sicily would play a fundamental role in my life. It was truly love at first sight, a love that over the years was to become ever deeper and eternal.
It is not my intention to write about my life, which would only be of moderate interest. Instead, I will try to draw the reader into the atmosphere that slowly but inexorably enveloped me over the years before my garden was born, and I will recount certain episodes and unique encounters that strengthened my bond to this enchanting land.

The Mafia boss

Once a year, in the middle of summer, my husband Scipione would have to go to Mussomeli to collect the quit rent on his mother's properties. This was rent on perpetual leases that was collected in kind and not in cash. This entailed a complicated set of rituals, which were overseen by Mr. Ferreri, for whom the 'guarantor' was Giuseppe Genco Russo, nicknamed 'Zu' Peppe' and the head of the Mafia at the time.
The summer of 1960 was particularly hot. It was August, and to get to Mussomeli from Palermo, where we lived, we had to drive over kilometres and kilometres of dusty roads. There were no straightaways except the one known as chianotta di Vicari, infamous as a place where it was easy to ambush travellers, as it was set at the bottom of a valley that could easily be watched from the surrounding hillsides. We set out on that road in a little two-

tone Fiat Seicento with a sunroof: we were white from the dust and baked by the sun. When we arrived in town, Scipione told me he had to attend to business with Mr. Ferreri for about half an hour, saying that I could take this opportunity to look around. Scipione's 'half hours' can stretch into hours, but curiosity prevailed over the prospect of having to sit and wait.

I was on a steep road paved with large sections of lava rock that formed a small gutter in the middle as a runoff for rain and wastewater. Along the side was an unbroken row of houses of different heights, with sloped tiled roofs set asymmetrically toward one side or the other. They had a central door, almost invariably painted green, that was divided across the middle so it could be used as both a window and main door, allowing people as well as animals to exit or look outside. A donkey with pointed ears and a resigned look poked out its grey head.

A little further ahead, a goat tied to an iron ring bleated insistently. One leaf of the door was open and two women dressed in black, seated with their curved backs to the road, were roasting peppers on a small iron stove reddened from the heat. The enticing scent of sweet spices was everywhere. The sky was layered with a blanket of heat so intense that it hid the blue, and time seemed to have come to a standstill.

I was holding a film camera I had brought with me for my first meanderings in the heart of Sicily, conquered by the violent appeal of those boundless landscapes, that series of sloping horizons and the colours, between ochre and pale yellow, of the crops that had been harvested long before.

Suddenly, the rhythmic beat of quick little footsteps made me stop and turn to see two enormous dark eyes, set deep in a grimy little face. A little boy of about six, barefooted and wearing a fad-

ed T-shirt over frayed shorts, stared at me in silence. When our eyes met, without saying a word he imperceptibly raised his chin to beckon me. I understood that I was supposed to follow him. He dashed off as if he had little wings on his feet and, curious, I hastened to follow him.
We arrived at a clearing at the end of town and before me was a slope that opened onto the valley, with the impressive and majestic castle of Chiaramontano in the middle. The little boy stopped and, ever silent, he looked up to show me the open door of a house behind us, and then he disappeared.
I was perplexed for a moment and then, crossing the threshold of the little two-storey house, I climbed two flights of narrow stone steps with immaculate whitewashed walls. I began to hear men's voices and had not reached the top of the last flight of stairs when a door opened and the silhouette of a woman, covered with a fringed black shawl, stepped back to let me in.
I entered a small rectangular room with a laid table in the centre and five men around it, all of whom had turned to face me: Scipione, who was smiling, perhaps over the curious look on my face, Mr. Ferreri, and two young men who kept somewhat to themselves. And in the middle, dressed in black with a dark cap on his head and a scarf wrapped around his neck twice, was Giuseppe Genco Russo.
There was a bowing and scraping, hand-kissing and a series of 'God bless Your Excellency', followed by a peremptory invitation to sit at the head of the table with the Boss on my right and the eldest of his two sons on my left. Scipione sat to the right of Genco Russo. Before each diner there wasn't just a plate but a stack of dishes with a bowl on top. Given the number, I understood that a difficult task awaited me, as I wasn't about to offend our host.

Scipione started by saying that he had a stomach ache and could barely eat, so the responsibility of making a good impression fell squarely on my shoulders. I was hungry, as usual, and I undertook the task of doing honour to the meal. Delicious soup to start, followed by pasta, lamb, cutlets, fried chicken, vegetables, cheese, and cakes – particularly large around here – filled with almond paste and chocolate. I was spared the fruit and the entire meal was accompanied by a young but full-bodied wine that was rosy red in colour and quite pleasant. I didn't bat an eye and, with a smile, I ate everything.

At the end of the meal, we got up and went out to the small terrace overlooking the valley.

The afternoon sun made the light softer and rosier, and the mountains, near and far, took on hues muted by thousands of nuances. I picked up my film camera and, focusing on Genco Russo, I said, 'Let me film you. In a while, you can come visit us and I'll show it to you'.

He frowned at me without saying a word, and then he called one of his grandchildren, took her by the hand, wrapped his scarf around him tightly so that even his mouth was almost covered and, with his cap still perched on his head, he struck a pose, immobile.

I filmed him for some time and then I turned to Scipione, saying, 'We should be getting back to Palermo. Dusk is about to fall'. Looking Genco Russo straight in the eye, I continued, 'It isn't wise to travel around here at night!'.

Those dark and penetrating eyes stared at me quizzically and then, laying his hand across his chest, he said in a deep voice, 'When Your Excellency leaves my house, there is nothing to worry about'. 'If you say so…,' I countered, barely smiling.

Six months later in our apartment in Palermo, toward the end of

a winter afternoon at the hour that Monica and Sofia would play with us after lunch, the doorman very excitedly announced over the intercom that 'Zu' Peppe' was asking to be received. A few minutes later, in came Giuseppe Genco Russo, black cap on his head, scarf, grandchildren at his side, a daughter-in-law and one of his sons, who was carrying an enormous tray of ladyfingers.
Without mincing words, before the stunned gaze of the girls the Boss asked me if they could see 'u filmo'. We quickly set up the screen, the projector and a row of chairs for the 'audience' that, in addition to the entire Genco Russo family, included Monica and Sofia, sitting stiffly in their red robes.
In an instant, the terrace of Mussomeli was before us and, in the foreground, there appeared the serious and penetrating gaze of 'Zu' Peppe' under the cap that seemed to be part of his head. He had a rather unpleasant habit: he would spit continuously into a huge white handkerchief.
He asked to see it again at least four times and a hint of a smile came over his otherwise sombre face. Then he suddenly stood up and kissed Scipione on both cheeks. Turning to me, he kissed my hand, mumbled 'God bless Your Excellency' and, silent family in tow, he left.

The promissory note

Caltanissetta is set high in the hills that overlook the Salso river valley, surrounded by honey-coloured fields dotted with Modicana cows that look like they're made of chocolate. It has its own quiet majesty, fully aware that it is the heart of Sicily, equidistant from the cities overlooking the sea: Palermo, Catania, Agrigento and Siracusa.
It wasn't easy to get there during the late Fifties. You had to take

impassable roads, said to have been marked out by the hooves of donkeys carrying salt-filled bags that had been pierced in order to leave a track behind, following the synclines of the mountains. It took hours by car, without air-conditioning back then, encountering only flocks of sheep and herds of cattle that never seemed to end. In the summer, the heat was so real you could almost reach out and touch it, in an immense and majestic landscape that spoke to you about this ancient and breathtaking land, laden with smells and sensations.

We went to live at the Hotel Concordia Mazzoni, an old nineteenth-century villa set in the middle of a lovely garden in the centre of town. Scipione had to meet sharecroppers, overseers, bank officers and attorneys. With regard to banks, I'll tell you a story that needs no further comment, and it will give you a good idea of the atmosphere during that period.

Scipione had to collect the money for a piece land rented to Ciccio Di Cristina, a 'uomo di panza', to use the Mafia argot, and an oft-cited figure in the news many years later.

Di Cristina didn't have enough money to pay what he owed, so he tried to have Scipione himself endorse a promissory note. The proposal was unacceptable. Scipione told him to return the next day, at eleven o'clock on the dot, to meet him at the office of the director of the bank that was still known then as the Cassa di Risparmio delle Province Siciliane.

The next day, Scipione arrived promptly at the appointment with Giuseppe Genco Russo at his side as the guarantor. The astonished bank director rose from his armchair, welcoming both 'the Prince' and 'Zu' Peppe' with the utmost respect and reverence, and without any discussion whatsoever he accepted that signature to back Di Cristina's promissory notes.

Scipione quickly discounted the notes, smiled hugely, and after much handshaking and reverent bowing on the others' part, he left.

The law office

Part of the Mazzone family lived at 19 Via Cavour, between the railroad station and the Hotel Concordia: Mrs. Lucia, Mrs. Lucia's mother, her daughter Mirella with her husband, an attorney by the name of Rosario Alessi but known to everyone as Saro, and their four children.

It was a solid three-storey house set on the corner, built in the local ochre-coloured stone at the end of the nineteenth century, and it had tall windows and an impressive front door. On the left side of the ground floor, there was a French door with the plaque of the law offices. When I opened the door, a little bell would jingle, making Mrs. Tripiciano, the secretary, look up from the typewriter. The bespectacled Mrs. Tripiciano had dark hair and a dark complexion and was dressed in black from head to toe.

I was particularly struck by the sheer blouse she wore, under which you could glimpse her slip, invariably black. I wondered if she harboured an unconscious desire to look attractive, a 'sexy look', as Saro would say with a laugh.

I had never been inside a provincial Sicilian law office before and I was immensely curious and pleased. The head of the office was the Hon. Giuseppe Alessi, an eminent criminal lawyer and later the President of the Region of Sicily during the Sixties, who went by the epithet of 'uncle'.

Saro asked me to follow him to his office and told me to take a seat in the armchair in the corner to watch his clients come and go.

A few minutes later, the tinkling of the front door was followed by Mrs. Tripiciano's announcement that the Di Castro family had arrived. In came the mother, the father, a plain-looking son and the daughter-in-law – all in mourning, the women wrapped in wide fringed shawls that hid most of their faces and their bodies, decidedly stout in both cases.

The men were wearing their Sunday best, a black button in their buttonholes, and they had thick moustaches and rough, tanned hands.

Mama's eyes were swollen from crying and she sobbed unashamedly, 'My son, my son! Attorney, you must sent his murderer to jail! He must grieve for the rest of his life – and not just him but his whole family'.

The men did their best to sustain her, whilst the daughter-in-law, pale and lost, did not dare to weep or speak and was somewhat removed from everything, as if the dead man no longer had anything to do with her and belonged once again only to his mother.

Saro waited for her crying to die down and asked the men for more detailed information about the tragedy, the possible motives for the murder, the alleged murderers, the place, the time and the date of the crime. It was difficult to understand anything, except for the fact that there was a woman involved who had caused the argument, and that perhaps this woman was the daughter-in-law. The decision was made to bring civil action against the alleged murderer and after discussing things for over an hour, the family left.

We had barely finished commenting on this visit when the arrival of a new client was announced.

This time, although she was dressed in dark clothes, the woman who entered the office wore a touch of colour. She wasn't in mourning for the time being and had a decisive and belligerent look, her eyes ablaze and her chin raised with an air of challenge.

She was followed by her husband, a short and stocky man whose shoes looked one size too big for him, and he gripped his cap nervously in his hands. Behind them was a young brown-haired woman with a light complexion who was quite buxom, making her attractive and appealing. She was neither shy nor candid, but there was something defiant in her eyes, as if she were ready to take on the world.

Addressing the attorney, the woman came straight to the point, virtually cutting him off. ‘Attorney, you must get my son out of jail. He’s a good boy and this disgraceful woman here was the one who drove him to shoot. Our family honour had to be saved’.

And out came a litany of reasons of all kinds to convince the lawyer that the crime that had been committed wasn’t really all that serious.

Saro listened attentively and when he was finally able get a word in, he turned to the mother and said, ‘Ma’am, I’ll see what I can do. But don’t forget that your son killed someone!’.

The woman was puzzled for a moment and then, looking at him squarely, she exclaimed, ‘Attorney! Dead is dead. Now we need to help the living!’.

Mourning

Across southern Italy, wearing mourning is an age-old custom. Things are changing now, but in Sicily thirty years ago, mourning was a goal, and familiarity with funerals, black garments and preparing the deceased for eternal life were an integral part of daily life.

I was young and I didn’t think about death very often. My father had always entreated me not to wear black if he died young, also assuring me that he would certainly depart this life before he turned fifty: he died at the age of ninety-five! He wanted us to be happy and carefree, and to consider the end of life as a natural occurrence, like birth.

When I moved to Sicily, I almost immediately had to face a very different concept of death, attend lengthy funerals and pay visits to the family of the deceased, in an odd atmosphere in which true grief was mingled with curiosity and a large dose of hypocrisy.

One day Scipione had to pay a visit to the new head of the Agricultural Department in Caltanissetta. He asked me to go with him and I enthusiastically agreed, curious as I am about different customs and habits. We entered through a large double door, one side of which was shut and had a big and very showy black bow hanging on it. The professor's apartment was nearly pitch-black and since we had come in from the strong sunlight outside, it took us a while before we were able to see anything. All the furniture was draped with black cloths.

We were shown into the professor's studio and he came toward us, bowing silently and motioning for us to take a seat. Scipione immediately started to talk about the issue he had come to discuss, while I quietly observed the figure across from me. Not only was he wearing a black suit, but his shirt, tie, armband and the covered button in his buttonhole were also black, almost as if, through those details, he wanted to make his mourning over his wife's recent death even more powerful. He did indeed look very gloomy, since his eyes, hair and longish beard were also dark. And suddenly a thought popped into my head and I had an overwhelming urge to laugh, mixed with terror over the idea of what would happen if the person in front of me were able to read my mind: I wondered what colour the professor's drawers were. Black or white? I pretended to sneeze, cough and choke before

Scipione's astonished stare and his counterpart's impassive attitude. Thank goodness our meeting was over and we left to 'see the sky again'!

The funeral

Early in the spring of 1975, a man we had met with some dear friends of ours, and who had also been quite kind to us, passed away. He was a somewhat coarse and seemingly brusque fellow, but he had a heart of gold and a very generous spirit. We were told that the funeral would be held in Acireale at 11 o'clock on a certain day.

Scipione told me that it was impossible for him to be at the funeral and that it was essential that I go. There was no getting out of it and so, with very little enthusiasm, in order to avoid going alone I arranged to meet my friend Mirella, who was coming in from out of town for the occasion.

It was cool and partly cloudy, and a treacherous northwest breeze made me shiver. I parked near the church, the exterior of which was adorned completely in black, with long, gold-fringed drapes. An icy feeling crawled up my spine as I entered.

I sat in a pew with Mirella and observed the large crowd dressed almost entirely in dark clothing. In the first few rows, I could see the family of the deceased, two young children dressed in black, and all the women wearing veils. The priest turned to the congregation for his homily and I was amazed to hear him thunder, 'Listen to me, brothers! When the wrath of God comes down upon you it is like a bolt of lightning that strikes the oak tree!'. And as he was saying this, he was pointing to the coffin draped in black.

I must confess that I was overcome by the instinct to knock on wood, and I was filled with a feeling of fear and awe. Later, when

the funeral was over, my friend said that we should go immediately to greet the family.
I had tears in my eyes and a lump in my throat: this always happens to me at funerals, even if the deceased was not a particularly close friend or relative.
Pushing ahead gently, before me I saw a woman covered from head to toe in black veils and I tearfully threw myself into her arms. I felt a firm nudge in my back and a voice whispering something to me. I pulled away from the woman and, somewhat irritated, I turned to Mirella. 'What's the hurry?', I said. 'Miki,' she whispered in my ear, 'She's not the wife!'.
Uncontrollable laughter rose in my throat and I hurried down the side aisle, almost running out of the church.

The mayor
It was a windy and broiling September, and the city of Palermo was overrun by the garbage that had piled up after days and days of the garbage collectors' strike. Not only were there piles of bags – large and small – on every street corner, but the sirocco was whirling all sorts of garbage about, making the air stifling and laden with the sickening smell coming from those rotting heaps. It was a real danger to public health, and the press was already talking about an invasion of rats and the onset of salmonella epidemics, expressing the hope that the military would step in to help.
No one did anything and we seemed destined to drown in garbage. I decided to send a clear message to Salvo Lima, who was the city mayor at the time.
I went to buy two large sheets of white tissue paper and a roll of shiny red ribbon. I took a bag of garbage from the balcony outside our kitchen and dumped it in the middle of the snowy white

sheets of paper, which I had lined with newspaper. I wrapped it up into a lovely parcel, taking great pains to make it look attractive, I tied it with the red ribbon and wrote the following message on a card:"Se a ciascun l'interno affanno si leggesse in fronte scritto, quanti mai che invidia fanno ci farebbero pietà – Metastasio".

I closed the envelope and on it I wrote the name and address of the mayor who, as many people knew, lived in one of the famous skyscrapers on Viale Lazio. Then at about 1:30 pm, I scrambled into my Seicento and sped toward the address on the envelope. Back then, there were no escorts or special guards, and so when the doorman saw a smiling and well-dressed young woman arrive with a 'gift', he wasn't at all suspicious. In fact, he greeted me politely and when I asked him if the mayor was home, he answered, 'He just went up'. 'Please,' I said, 'give him this parcel. It's a surprise!'. And off I went, laughing.

I found out that the package was opened at the dinner table….

The next day, out of fear that Lima would blame the gesture on someone who had had nothing to do with it, I let him know through his trusted friends that I had been the one to bring the gift. I met him a few weeks later at the Teatro Massimo and he looked at me somewhat puzzled, but didn't say anything.

The strike finally came to an end and Palermo slowly went back to normal.

Friendship

I met Cesare Brandi in Palermo during the Sixties. I was fascinated by his vast knowledge and wit, never pedantic and always stimulating and varied. He loved Sicily and it was he who taught me to love it even more, who helped me experience the profound charm that this land, so full of contradictions, was able to impart. Through his words, I learned to see hidden treasures, hear melodious sounds and breathe in heady perfumes.

I saw Palermo in a light that was so full of splendour that I managed to close my eyes to all the atrocities and ugliness that the political class, ignorant, uneducated and dishonest as it was during those years, had managed to perpetrate. The plains of Piana dei Colli, a lovely and delightful stretch of lemon and orange groves that emanated their scent of the Orient in the evening, was systematically encroached upon by concrete and by horrible and poorly built skyscrapers, human beehives whose foundations were said to hide dozens of bodies.

Fortunately, the heart of the old city managed to escape this: the Mafia invaded the areas around it and the splendid eighteenth-century villas were suffocated beyond belief, but it was never able to lay its hands on the incredible cultural heritage of this unique and regal capital city. We would walk for hours with Brandi, discovering what so many and different cultures had left behind. Perhaps this was the reason it was so hard for me to leave when fate took me to another corner of Sicily, not all that far from Palermo but utterly different in its countryside and its people.

My friendship with Cesare Brandi didn't flag and he would often come to visit us in eastern Sicily, where we had moved. Scipione and I strolled with him to see the Baroque artwork of Noto, Modica and Scicli. We walked amidst the grey and reddish stones of the Necropolis of Pantalica, and together we explored Ferla, Solarino, Vizzini and Militello Val di Catania.

Wherever we went, we found kind and attentive guides who would open churches, oratories, convents and buildings. We never failed to try the local food, joke about the people we met and

go into raptures over the colours of the natural countryside, so varied and so different around every bend.
We lost Cesare Brandi too early: he died as a result of a fall in Palermo, dragged to the ground by a boy trying to steal his wallet. He never fully recovered and passed away after a long period of suffering.
The memory of his friendship and of his warm and wonderful long letters, written in his small and slanted hand, is something very precious that has never faded over the years.

The history

Cesare Brandi was the first to realise that the places around Case del Biviere, where we had been living for only a few years, were starting to change. One day, as we strolled amidst the first plants that were trying to bud in my fledgling garden, he said, 'Miki, your garden seems to have been born by magic!'.
Its magic was the magic of myth, of the legend it recounts, and this may be what makes it so evocative.
Myth or legend, Diodorus Siculus told the story of the lake of Hercules.
It is said that the first dam was built by the Knights Templar in order to keep the level of the lake from dropping too far. At times, the dam could also be opened to let in the barges that would sail up the river San Leonardo to load wheat.
During the Arab period, the name was changed to *Veverè*, fish hatchery, then to *Bevere* and finally Biviere. For the Arabs, the lake was very important because of its abundance of fish. They perfected a rather unique fishing system that took advantage of the predominant wind in the area, the west wind.
The water and fish that flowed into the deep channels, dug by

man in a reef of tufaceous rock, and ended up in chambers with many chambers, carved out of the rock. The water would flow off through a ceiling of woven reed mats, and the fish were stored in tanks and then sent to nearby markets.

Part of a very profitable feud, the lake covered an area of about 1300 hectares. As I mentioned in the introduction, in 1392 King Martin granted it to one of the ancestors of the Prince Branciforte of Butera, who married Johanna of Austria in about 1700 and went to live in Militello Val di Catania, a mountain village about 20 kilometres from the lake.

He was an attentive and farseeing proprietor and he took care of the unique lake flora as well as the fauna, which boasted of a rich variety of rare birds.

The lake of Biviere is referred to extensively in Sicilian literature: Pirandello mentions it in his short story *La roba*, Giovanni Verga and Quasimodo talk about it, and the contemporary author Turi Vasile cites it with a great sense of nostalgia.

From the few black-and-white photographs of the Thirties, it is easy to glean the great charm of these places and there is enormous regret over the loss of such an important body of water in an area with as little rainfall as Sicily, for which water is a precious resource.

In the nineteenth century, malaria started to become a serious problem for the populations living near the lake and the idea of draining it began to be discussed. It was not until 1930, the era of complete reclamation, that the decision was made to drain it and work began. Due to the war, it was not completed until the Fifties. The Region of Sicily issued a special expropriation law and a large part of the reclaimed land was taken from its owners and assigned to fishermen.

Arrival

At the end of 1967 Scipione and I were to make the decision that changed our lives completely.

We arrived in Biviere with our four small children and our idea was to transform this place, which no longer had any water or vegetation, into a farm where we would plant citrus groves and sow durum wheat.

'Case del Biviere' – which means the 'houses of Biviere' – was essentially a small village to the east of the erstwhile lake. The houses had been uninhabited for years and were in bad shape. Grey inside with barracks-style paint, they were the refuge of mice and cockroaches.

The only thing to do was to avoid getting depressed, consider myself a pioneer, roll up my sleeves and try to turn an uninhabitable spot into a place to live.

One rainy day, I decided to devote my time to decorating the windows of our bedrooms, which were as grey and ugly as the rest of the house, once the headquarters of the Reclamation Consortium.

Donning rubber boots, a hunting jacket and a felt hat, and carrying an enormous green umbrella to stay dry, I went to Lentini to find a haberdashery to buy needles, thread and notions. I was told to go to a wooden door on the south side of Piazza del Duomo and, closing my umbrella as I crossed the threshold, I walked into the vestibule. The shrill buzzing of the voices stopped suddenly and I noticed that all the women, wrapped in long black shawls, had turned their eyes to me in surprise, questioning me.

Their heads moved in unison to scrutinise me, starting with my feet and then moving up slowly to take in the rest of me. I was dismayed.

After a few seconds, the shop owner, a thin and wiry woman, addressed me with a shout:
'Foreigner?'
I didn't say a word and simply shook my head.
All eyes started to move up and down and, in a crescendo, the haberdasher hissed:
'Actress?'
Never speaking, I shook my head as irrepressible laughter began to rise in my throat. Now everyone was puzzled and astonished. The woman stared at me at length, and then her face suddenly brightened and, pointing her finger at me, she confidently cried:
'The circus!'
I hurried off, without any needles or thread, laughing to myself.
A month later, I decided to try my luck again, hoping that I would no longer have an identity problem, as gossip flies through these towns like the wind. I stopped again at the threshold of the shop and this time, I looked the owner squarely in the eye.
She recognised me immediately and with a sweeping gesture toward the women there, she boomed, 'Make way, you idiots, make way'.
Once again, she took me by surprise and made me feel very ill at ease.
'I can wait, miss. I'm not in a hurry', I said.
'Why didn't you tell me who you are?', she asked me, almost in dismay. 'Your Excellency, please come in. At your service'.
I bought a lot of things as fast as I could so I wouldn't make those who had arrived before me wait too long and then, smiling to myself, I went home.

Heaven on earth

The early years at Case del Biviere came and went peacefully. We were surrounded by our four beautiful children, Monica, Sofia, Maria Neve

and Giangiacomo, who were happy to live in the country, go around on their bicycles, use the swing we'd strung up between two cypresses on the side of the chapel and traipse through the fields to watch their first threshing, treading barefooted in the wheat or seated atop a large tractor ploughing the land.
For them, this was heaven on earth. They wore jeans and boots, and lived alongside cats, dogs, geese, the henhouse and a donkey named Agatha, not to poke fun at the saint venerated in Catania but at a dull and vexing middle-aged 'sitter'.
One day, we even adopted a ewe. After a terrible night in which stray dogs wreaked havoc in our well-supplied henhouse, the children helped me set up a field hospital for the chickens, with rows of wooden crates where we laid out the injured and those that had survived the massacre.
One of these was the henhouse rooster, which we found lying on the ground half-dead, its neck stretched as long as a swan's. We curled it up in a crate, setting its neck in the proper position and holding it in place with a sort of armature of wooden splints. For many days, we used an eyedropper to feed it water and vitamins, until it was finally able to walk again on its own.
We named it January, because that was the month the massacre took place and – amazingly – after a while we heard it crowing again, discovering that it had once again taken over its role as the head of the henhouse!
It died of old age because not one of us had the courage to wring its neck twice, and it became our mascot.

Case del Biviere

As you come through the gate at the entrance, you see three buildings: the main house, the chapel dedicated to St. Andrew, patron saint of fishermen, and the inn where the hunters would spend the night as they awaited the dawn. The plaster is a rosy apricot colour with a warm tone reminiscent of oranges. These buildings were restored in their current layout after the terrible earthquake of 1693 that destroyed eastern Sicily., The restoration work was already finished by 1694, which is the date that is chiselled into the façade of the chapel over the coat of arms of the owner Branciforte, Prince of Butera. Set close together, the buildings are positioned asymmetrically to each other, almost like the wings of a stage.

In 1968, these houses had very few plants around them. A row of cypresses along the side of the chapel of St. Andrew, a hackberry (referred to by the Tuscans as spaccasassi or 'stone-splitter' and as melicucco by the Sicilians) across from the entrance, three *Schinus molle* or false peppers near the gate and six tree-trained acacia saligna on the western side, planted in large, ugly, triangular flowerbeds lined with cement, the outcome of the graceless imagination of the overseer back then.

The façade of the main house was masked by four enormous pillars in reinforced concrete that supported iron girders, and the overheated vines climbed up in an attempt to shade the entry. A lovely lone *Cereus spachianus* completed the flora of the vast now-deserted land around Case del Biviere. Dust and pebbles and not soil and stones. It was as if the water that had been diverted elsewhere to drain the lake had taken offence and forever abandoned this spot, once so famous for the flora and fauna that had lived here for centuries with water and for water.

The house, the port, the inn, the church all had that neglected look of little-loved places, empty and soulless. What was I to do? And where was I to begin?

At first, whenever I had a chance I would sit on the steps leading from the house to the area on the west, fascinated by the colours of the sunset and by a subtle yet perceptible feeling of peace, and I would ponder my surroundings. An invisible presence would sit next to me – perhaps the divine Ceres who, turning her gaze sadly toward those flatlands now devoid of water, was grieving for her legendary lake.
I liked to think that since we couldn't afford architects or landscape designers, we would have to rely on my imagination, and very little on what I knew.
I began to imagine a garden of green, sloping gently to the west as if it were chasing the very last sunbeam. I pictured thousands of shades, from the palest almost silvery green of the groundsels to the deep green of the cypresses, the only trees set all in a row near the chapel.
I could see big flowering bushes crowning the spaces that were left empty.

The dream starts to take shape
I began to read, and I discovered that the garden arose with man. Cavemen lived in a natural garden they learned to circumscribe, to enclose in order to prove their ownership. When the first rudimentary tools for agriculture were made during the Neolithic, the garden was invented. The word comes from the Hebrew gan and the Arabic gianna. The Paradise of the book of Genesis was the gan-eden and the Persian *pairidaeza*, the place that delights the eyes and nose. Just think of the gardens of Babylon, Ancient Egypt, China and Asia Minor.
The impressive Greek temples were set in the middle of extraordinary rock gardens rich in Mediterranean plants with penetrat-

ing scents. The Roman world surrounded itself with luxuriant gardens where water and plants intermingled. Different birds and animals lived there freely, like the ones we can see in the splendid mosaics at Villa del Casale in Piazza Armerina in Sicily, in the ruins unearthed in Pompeii and Herculaneum in Campania, and at Hadrian's Villa just outside Rome. Exotic plants from faraway countries adapted to our climate and today, centuries later, they are part of the Mediterranean flora.

I consider the garden the exterior continuation of the home. The large Renaissance gardens, with their geometries and their topiary art, would have no meaning without the grandeur of the residences and the large turreted villas as a backdrop. Those stone figures that populate the formal garden, the benches, the capitals, the balustrades and the parterres are the inhabitants and furnishings that have been brought outdoors to recreate the austere interior architecture. There is a profound symbiosis between the palazzo and the park: each would be incomplete without the other.

The same thing happens in the informal garden, the English garden, where geometry is virtually inexistent in order to make room for imagination, colour, a sense of space and fragrances.

The villas set in such different gardens are less imposing, their colours complement the flowering bushes. And flowering trees, citrus trees planted in the ground, big colourful bushes, vines and – depending on the latitude – extravagant succulent plants predominate, green statues that take the place of the stone ones.

In my dream, this was the garden I wanted to try to create, and one of the reasons was that I never wanted to forget the mythological origin of these places.

The beginning

I often felt discouraged, because it would have been far different if I had found an untended and abandoned garden that had left a trace, a pattern to follow, plants to save. Instead, I found myself facing a broad stretch of dried mud dotted with stones. And yet those stones spoke to me and sparked something in my mind.

One spring afternoon, I went with Scipione and our four children to visit a nursery on the outskirts of Acireale. It felt like heaven on earth to me, and it seemed that all the flora of the world was represented in that little space. I didn't know the botanical names, the species or the families, and I felt lost. I looked at everything and bought a few little succulents, but what enchanted me was a little lone plant in a terracotta pot. It was a dark-green plant with fleshy leaves set in a rosette, which an unknown painter had edged in white with imaginative little smudges.

Some time later, a few friends came for lunch, which we had laid out on impromptu tables and chairs. The air shone with blue and with sunshine. Everything had been washed and cleaned, the tablecloths were the colour of sunflowers and the enamel-blue dwarf irises, which the children and I had picked in the middle of the rocks behind the house during a long walk, were our cheerful and charming centrepieces. And in pots set all in a row, the little plants I had bought in Acireale encouraged each other, aware that they were pioneers in this place with such little greenery.

Our friend Ettore, a botany expert, looked at them all with a gentle and somewhat compassionate smile… and then he spied my little white-painted friend. He stopped and asked me, 'May I have this? It's an Agave victoria regina and it's quite rare'.

'I'm sorry, I can't. It's the only rare plant I own! But you can come see it whenever you like'.

This seemingly unimportant episode may well have been a decisive moment in the destiny of the garden of Case del Biviere.
The next day, as I looked around once again to find a corner suitable for transplanting my little friend, I looked closely at the long jetties of the ancient port, built with huge squared rocks hewn long ago from the nearby tuff quarries.

The idea
There they were, tired of being useless after centuries of long service supporting and sheltering wooden boats that narrowed to a point fore and aft, and the wide quarare made of black iron and covered with pitch. The jetties were the silent and powerful witnesses of the laborious life of the fishermen, basket-weavers and blacksmiths. They had been built on a large rocky bank on the east side of the lake, Hercules' legendary lake surrounded by hills and mountains, with the snow-capped mass of Mongibello dominating the horizon to the north. A fabulous landscape, loved and lost.
Those abandoned jetties no longer had any reason to be, for there was no water to be contained nor boats to host. And yet it seemed to me that a voice was asking me not to remove them but to try to use them. I imagined two long beds of succulent plants in an array of varieties and sizes, breathing life and colour back into the splendid grey and red rocks.
The idea came to me suddenly, and my imagination was carried away with it: I would bring those places of ancient memories back to life and give them a new reason to exist. The allure of abandoned vestiges is the allure of the past, the mystery of death. What was needed here was life. From now on, there would be soil, trees, bushes and flowers where there once had been reeds, lake vegetation and water.

The jetties would hold succulent plants with strange shapes, like green and cerulean sculptures looking up to the heavens – and with them, my little *Victoria regina*.
Dreams... and an enormous amount of work.

The garden is born
The opportunity to start putting things in order came a short time later. A lorry driver who was working on the construction of the motorway to Ragusa asked Scipione for a place to dump the dirt the bulldozers were digging. It was certainly not woodland soil and the dirt that, lorry after lorry, was being dumped in the large empty spaces left after the water had been drained looked like potter's clay.
Once the area had been filled, the earth levelled and the stones of the jetties brought to the surface and compacted, we could start to see a layout. The jetties, about a metre and a half wide and approximately thirty metres long, were filled with round basalt rocks. We had some of them removed and filled the space with the black and humus-rich soil of Biviere.
The first succulents began to arrive. We went everywhere – to markets and nurseries – to buy the unfamiliar and nameless little plants that were so different from each other. And wherever we went, botanical and private gardens alike, we asked if we could take a fleshy leaf, a spiny shoot, a new bud. Nothing could stop our pressing desire to see those extraordinary flowerbeds come back to life. Thus, we set the first little plants in a raised, well-drained, bright and fertile bed.
Little by little, over the months and years, the jetties became populated with marvellous living forms that were united by their extraordinary capacity to adapt to the temperature swings that

are so frequent in our climate, using their flesh and water-rich structure as they like during the long dry spells.
While we were taking a walk around Lentini, we discovered the dry bed of a creek filled with round white stones. The children were excited about collecting them, and for days we filled our baskets with these stones, a goldmine for separating an *opuntia* from an *aloe*, a *cereus* and a *mammillaria.*
As if by magic, day by day the two long jetties were gradually populated with dozens of extraordinary denizens, tall and slender, short and round, thorny, pointy, trailing, hanging. Anyone who has learned to love the strange world of 'succulent plants' knows that with them – perhaps more so than with any other botanical genus – nature unleashed its imagination, giving almost architectural shapes to these odd inhabitants of the planet. They are prudent, careful, jealous plants, made only to be admired and not touched. I must confess that I have underestimated their defensive systems more than once, regretting my gloves, tools and precautions. On the other hand, they are not very demanding: plenty of light, good drainage and abundant water only during the hottest months. And then they grow quickly – healthy, silky and exuberant.
The first year was very disappointing: most of my plants died after a winter of continuous frosts. Discouraged and depressed, I was dismayed to see the disaster wreaked by the frost and almost lost my enthusiasm.
'I don't have a green thumb,' I declared, but my Sardinian roots had the upper hand. I stubbornly decided to start again and suddenly I had an idea: I would cover each little plant using a flask with the straw removed and the bottom cut off, making little personal greenhouses that let in light, the sun, but not the cold.

The planting continues

An unusual and entertaining sight appeared on the jetties: the plants would peep out, protected but illuminated, and would peacefully observe the winter from their verandas. Several large demijohns were ideal for safeguarding some of the larger specimens. It was a complete success and all of them survived the following winter.

In June of 1969, a lorry full of plants arrived from Palermo. Rosolino, the gardener from Villa Trabia who had fifty years of experience with unusual plants from faraway countries, came along in order to bed them. We were all very excited and the children enjoyed watching the work, always offering to hold the watering hose in their little hands.

Four small *Phoenix canariensis*, the lovely boulevard palms you see in many Italian cities that enjoy a temperate climate and around the entire Mediterranean basin, were set in large holes prepared the day before near the north entrance, and they were given plenty of water. June is the best month to transplant palm trees and the secret is to drown them with water.

It was the beginning of this oasis…!

About twenty trees were planted here and there outside the little port: young elms, pruned and a bit ugly, which after being planted, gave more of the impression of a memorial park than a budding garden. And all that bare greyish soil, ploughed roughly, gave me a feeling of desolation.

Then came the turn of the *Yucca elephantipes*, which immediately imparted a sense of stability. Their wrinkled feet, reminiscent – as the name implies – of those of pachyderms, symbolise longevity, strength and vigour.

Their young, long, stiff and pointed leaves, which are a lovely bright green, were turned skyward, constantly seeking light and warmth.
I understood that this was the right place for them. The empty old port was slowly being transformed into a 'verdant harbour', to use the words written years later by an Irish visitor, landscape architect Patrick Bowe. He was enchanted by this green port with large *Yucca elephantipes* rising from it, planted against the jetties almost as if they were imposing and towering sailing ships at their mooring.
Today, more than thirty years later, they have become giants with a powerful base, and their tops are covered with long inflorescences of dozens of little white bells, ready to start a cheerful concert on the hot summer nights.

The Queen Mother
In March of 1988 we went to China with a group of new friends and stayed nearly a month. It was an incredible, paradoxical, amusing and highly instructive trip. There, I learned about a world far different from our own, discovering landscapes that looked as if they had been painted on silk and bonsai gardens circled with carved stones, terraces, dragons and mythical figures. We saw enormous rivers, the Great Wall, the great army of terracotta figures, large squares and rounded mountain chains.
Upon our return, we invited the entire group to come to Sicily in June, almost as a way of drawing a comparison between our sunny landscape and the damp fog we had crossed together.
When we got back to Rome, where our children – adults by now and some of whom were married – had been living for several years, at lunchtime there was a telephone call from London. A

gracious man wanted to know if we would be willing to receive the Queen Mother at Biviere in June, as she was very interested in visiting our garden.

I was speechless, and I immediately though it must be a practical joke or a case of mistaken identity, but it wasn't. As a result, in May there was an inspection by the British consul in Naples (for the English, the Kingdom of Two Sicilies still exists), together with the head of the queen's private police corps, and together we established everything, from the menu to the duration of the visit.

Satisfied, they left, and in May we received an invitation to dine aboard the *Britannia* moored at the port of Catania, on the evening of 19th June. It was a special evening, with the Queen Mother dressed in pink chiffon bedecked with splendid jewels, and we sat in a dining room filled with travel mementos, including the solid gold centrepiece sent by the Sultan of Kuwait.

The next day, 20th June, at exactly twelve o'clock the royal Rolls Royce came through the gate, followed by numerous cars with guests, the Carabinieri corps, the State Police and bodyguards. A minor army set up camp on the sidelines as the Queen Mother, dressed in light blue from head to toe, smiled sweetly as she got out of the car. The first one to greet her was our little grandson Giacomo, who gave her a bouquet of pink roses that had been picked for her minutes before.

Then we introduced our children, all our 'Chinese' friends and several people we had invited for the occasion. We also welcomed the Queen's personal guests and the British ambassador to Italy.

The Queen Mother was a very gracious and charming person who is young in spirit, and she was delighted to see the *Xanthorrea arborea*, which had blossomed in her honour (it blooms every ten years), the jacarandas with a periwinkle carpet at their feet, and

the *Parkinsonia aculeata*, a cloud of yellow flowers that smell like jasmine.
She walked around the whole garden for an hour, protecting herself from the Sicilian sun, which is already quite hot in June, with an old white parasol. She asked for explanations about all the plants, bushes and succulents. The proprietress of breathtaking gardens, she was enchanted by ours, which was very young but already full of magic.
We had organised a luncheon for forty people in the area near the swimming pool. There were four round tables seating ten people each, set with lovely white damask linen tablecloths and napkins embroidered with a crown, all the work of Monica and her workshop 'Fiordilino'.
The centrepieces were different: the Queen's was composed entirely of pink Queen Elizabeth roses and it was set with the blue, red and pink dinnerware from the East India Company. The centrepieces on the other tables were pyramids of lemons mixed with blue irises, and they were set with green and white Wedgwood dishes.
The Queen Mother was delighted with our menu, particularly the cheese mousse and the vanilla ice cream served with a warm sauce of bitter orange marmalade.
She was sorry to leave and when she signed our guest book, she left us a lovely autographed and framed photograph.
The next year, she sent her grandson, the Prince of Wales. Dressed in jeans and a shirt, he had lunch with us, sitting on the terrace overlooking the garden, and when he returned to England he wrote me a long and warm letter of thanks. The following May, I was invited to Clarence House for tea and lunch, and I accompanied the Queen Mother to the inauguration of the Chelsea Show amidst a profusion of flowers.

We realised then that the garden could be open to nature-lovers who wanted to see a place that had held nothing a few years before and had gradually become a delightful and lush oasis.
Many visitors have come and gone, some of whom are quite famous, such as the King and Queen of Belgium, art critics, film directors, actors, writers, journalists, architects and many Italian and foreign enthusiasts who have written reminiscences, comments and impressions.
The appendix includes the words of some of the people who perceived the hidden soul of 'the garden that wasn't' and that now rewards us with its presence at every moment.

The guided tour

Let's imagine we're taking one of the many groups of Italians or foreigners who cross the gate at the entrance each year on a guided tour of the garden.
I usher them into the lovely and cool chapel of St. Andrew, where they are welcomed by Gramignani's beautiful painting, commissioned by the lord of the estate in 1757 and depicting the *Pesca miracolosa.* Here, I tell my visitors the mythical story of the lake, the fishing trade, how it was drained, and the birth of the garden. The visitors listen quietly and attentively, and they begin to sense the atmosphere surrounding us.
We leave the chapel and set out on our tour of the park. Just to the right of the door, an extraordinary specimen of a *Dasylirion longissimus* flutters and sparkles. In the spring of 2001, it blossomed for the very first time, with a long dark-red inflorescence that was absolutely spectacular: a real botanical experience, as it blossoms only once every ten years!
Opposite this is an impressive *Xanthorrea arborea* in a reclining

position, as if it were the Paulina portrayed at the Borghese Gallery. During the Seventies, the pillars in reinforced concrete that concealed the simple but charming design of the façade were knocked down one by one, and four grapefruit trees were planted on the terrace overlooking the entrance to the house. In the more sheltered corner, we planted a *Euphorbia canariensis* that is now as tall as the roof.

A few years ago, we added five cactuses along the façade. Each one is different in both shape and size and, set in square stone flowerbeds filled with white pebbles, they look like tall guardians protecting our home.

The *Aloe comosa*, with its fleshy pea-green leaves, stands alone at the end of the east jetty, facing a vigorous *Cereus spachianus* whose enormous pinkish-white flowers open for just a few hours, as if by magic.

We pass by the *Nolina Beaucarnea*, which was tiny the year we planted it. Now it shows off with its five ruffled branches, climbing onto the little terrace overlooking the port with the ancient bronze bell from Burgio, the town in the province of Agrigento famous for its bells. With its deep, solemn chimes, it would alert the fishermen, busy working at the lake, that it was time for Mass. Today, it is covered with a hat of white-and-green ivy, intertwined with the thorny branches of an *Alberique Barbier* rosebush and the fleshy ones of a *Solandra major*.

The two plane trees

In the middle of the port, there are two plane trees with a curious history. They were planted very young, the one on the right in the spot where it can be seen today, and the one on the left between the two jacarandas near the east jetty.

One of the most common errors made by beginning gardeners is to bed plants too close together, without considering their future growth and the amount of room needed by large trees. After a few years, the two jacarandas showed obvious signs of intolerance toward the young plane tree planted between them, and they began to bend – one to the right and the other to the left – to avoid it. The message was clear and we decided to transplant the 'unwelcome guest' so it would be aligned with its big brother, calling to mind two large sailing ships riding at anchor in the middle of the port. Our second arrival was short and lean, with an odd wrinkly trunk that was nothing like its twin's lovely squamous trunk.
It didn't waste any time, always competing to match its companion in height and vigour. Oddly enough, however, its young branches lost the wrinkled appearance of the trunk to acquire the same unique feature as the plane tree on the right: the scaly spots. Several botany professors from the University of Palermo explained that the tree had undergone a sort of root symbiosis with its neighbours during their close coexistence. As a result, even today, up to a certain height plane tree number two has maintained a wrinkly trunk similar to the one of the two graceful jacarandas. Over in a corner, an enormous oleander as white as snow has a bright pink branch, and its dazzling blooms delight us all summer long. Across from it, in order to give us springtime blossoms, there is a large *Fortuniana* rosebush, a Banxia that thrives only in hot countries. At the beginning of May, it is covered with thousands of little white pompons all in a row down its hanging branches: a breathtaking sight that has our visitors in raptures.

The west garden

We leave the green port and pass under an arch made of lava

stone to go to the west side: a sunny impact, a luxuriant lawn and a terrace with a balustrade set in a forest of green. Red bougainvillea climbs to crown the wrought-iron arches, and there's a *Yucca aloifoliæ marginata*, with its pointed green and yellow heads that are often so heavy they drop down onto the lawn to form an enormous spiky bush.

We encounter a huge *Furcrea selloa*, an agavacea with long leaves as stiff as swords, the *Solandra major* that also flowers in the middle of winter, with its large funnel-shaped mustard-yellow blossoms and leaves that are often a beautiful glossy green, the sweet-smelling *Stephanotis*, a slow climber with clusters of white flowers, and the gigantic *Euphorbia grandidens* guarding the left-hand balustrade. A new *Lonicera caprifolium* plant adds its delicate perfume to this corner of tropical paradise.

To the left of the stairs leading to the house, we come across the extraordinary *Corysia*, with its bottle-shaped trunk covered with big round thorns. It is known as a 'false kapok', because its ripe berries yield plenty of silky cotton hiding black seeds that germinate readily.

Rising to the left, feathery and solitary, there was an extraordinary *Parkinsonia aculeata* that a tornado uprooted and knocked down in October of 1999. Now its roots have started to sprout again and these shoots are already tall and vigorous. Perhaps a few years from now we will again enjoy the unrivalled show of its June flowering, when it is covered with very fragrant clusters of yellow flowers and long, slender, downy leaves.

The English named the plant in honour of Mr. Parkinson, a botanical artist the English court sent to Australia on one of

Captain Cook's ships. Parkinson, who died during the journey home, went to look for exotic plants and seeds to bring home in order to acclimate them in the royal greenhouses.
In the wall that separates the port from the western area, a niche carved in the stone holds a lovely column of blond marble with the bust of Ceres, smiling sweetly and looking – in satisfaction, I hope – at the transformation undergone by her mythical lake.

Around the swimming pool
Before we go down the two stone stairs leading to the lower part of the garden, along the sides of the sloping embankments we encounter a long row of plants and herbs, starting with the *Poinciana* or *Bonapartea*, with its red moustache circling its bright yellow inflorescences and its sensitive little leguminous leaves.
There is a young and hardy specimen of *Aloe bainesii*, and then a *Yucca speciosa* I've renamed 'serpentine' because of the atypical bearing of its prostrate and snake-like trunk that continues to sprout new plants. This was a gift from the director of the botanical garden of Mahé in the Seychelles.
An *Agave americana striata* that looks like it was painted by an impatient artist came from the botanical garden of Ottonella on the island of Elba, owned by our friend Sandro Bronzini Zapelloni.
The *Orocereus celsianus*, a cactus covered with ruffled white hair, sits in a beautiful eighteenth-century Caltagirone vase. There is a column-like *Lemaiocereus marginatus*, alongside numerous *Cotyledon orbiculata* bushes, with their fat and fleshy leaves.
And we must not forget the roses: an astonishing bush of pearly, *Sea, foam*, roses, embracing, *Pelargonium, citronel-*

la bush from the beautiful garden of Castello Pisani Dossi in Como, the fuchsia *Castor* and *Pollux* roses, the dark purple *Cardinal Richelieu* mingled with the *Clair matin*, and a dazzling *Carissa* with fleshy leaves and the scent of jasmine. These roses and the *Carissa* have become entwined with the yuccas, the agaves and the aloes, changing their appearance to make them more colourful and graceful, and not quite as stiff and spiky.

I think this mingling of the plants makes the garden more cheerful and varied, albeit less orderly and perfect. It enhances its charm.

On the west side of the pool are two enormous groups of *Washingtonia robusta* with 5 and 6 trunks, which we planted when our first grandson Giacomo was born in 1984. They are the daughters of the first little plant, and I have saved the little oblong terracotta vase that held it when my friend Umberta Patrizi, who owns a garden in the Roman countryside that is famous for its roses, gave it to me in 1978.

Just ahead is an extraordinary specimen of Cereus Jamacaru, solemn and majestic, which blossoms on summer nights with big white and yellow flowers, and I've swathed it in a cloud of jasmine.

At the bottom of the stairs leading to the swimming pool, an uncommonly large *Agave ferox* comes into view. Its colour, the deepest green, and its fleshy leaves, toothed with insidious claws and a tip that can pierce you like a stiletto, make it one of the specimens most commonly photographed by visitors.

Nearby, the Roman anchor that Scipione discovered in the waters of Porto Ercole rests against two enormous stones from the ancient port, and it looks like a large grey bird, wings outspread as if it were about to fly away.

Meeting the plants

We stroll under the *Phoenix canariensis*, with leaves so long they touch the ground and form a cool green vault even during the long summer days scorched by the sun. The two lemon trees between them, always laden with lovely yellow fruit, remind us that we are in the land that Goethe, during his travels through Italy, called 'Das Land wo di citronen blumen'. On summer nights, the scent of lemon blossoms is mingled with the perfume of jasmine. The *Dracena draco* is still young, but it already has dozens of branches that flower each year, sprouting new heads. It rests against an arch made of lava rock that leads to a large canopy shaded by a reed roof. Solitary and majestic, a greyish-green *Agave salmiana*, which has leaves that look like canoes and have the consistency of leather, has reigned for years near the arches of climbing roses, only to begin blossoming in a long stele that seems to want to touch the sky. Perhaps you didn't know that after it blossoms, the agave dies, and in its long agony it showers all its extraordinary energy to its growing child, to make it as lovely and spectacular as possible. The agave withers day by day, its leaves shrink and dry out as its stele opens its branches like a candelabra, crowning them with silky, fluttery flowers that, in turn, will be transformed into dozens of tiny new plants: a heartrending swansong in a death that is eternal rebirth.

We keep walking and encounter the *Encephalartos horridus*, a *cycadacea* that is found in the forests of South Africa. Fossils of this plant have been found in various areas on our planet. We received it in 1989 for Scipione's birthday.

The *Glaedischia* is an Australian leguminosa that, in its original habitat, covers its trunk with long ruby-coloured spines to protect itself against the danger of squirrels and other rodents that love to eat its tasty flowers.

Then we have twin *Cocos plumosa*, feathery and light, the groups of *Cycas revoluta*, the *Callystemon coccinea*, the *Philodendron selloum*, an exuberant *Phitolacca dioica*, and the tall *Populus tremulus*, known as 'Moroccan birch' because of its ash-white trunk etched with dark colours.
Let's keep going: we come to a lovely bush of *Jasmine Grand Duke of Tuscany*, across from a young but dignified and impressive *Ficus magnoloides*, and a *Ceratonia siliqua*, the locust from the rocky areas around Ragusa that grows slowly, but with a hearty and self-satisfied air.
In the background, there are big islands of olive trees with a barrier of climbing roses behind them. The roses separate us from a hectare of palm trees we planted when they were very little, almost by chance, and they now look like a forest of foliage fluttering with every breeze.

Cool respite
Along the horizon are the gently sloping hills of Francofonte, Scordia and Militello, and the long road lined with *Pinus pineæ* marking off the southern end, whilst to the north is majestic Etna, the great snow-capped mountain with its curl of smoke. Magical Sicily, which stuns us with the scent of orange blossoms in April.
I can't forget the bougainvillea in so many different shades of red: deep violet, fiery red, pale lilac and orange. This year, a white one has also arrived, and we have sheltered it from the northern winds.
That fiery red rests on the covered area near the swimming pool, hanging down to the ground laden with clusters of coloured leaves.

We spend long hours there in the summer, cheered by the incursions of grandchildren and friends seeking cool respite from the sun in the turquoise water. The enormous stones that were used to mill wheat and rice, cultivated along the banks of the lake, are a welcome invitation to sit in the shade. The ancient stones give us a feeling of coolness even just by touching them, and they remind us of the lake.

To keep the past alive in this garden born from the waters, I have preserved a round boat with a diameter of about two metres. This flat-bottomed boat, made of iron painted with black pitch, was used by the canniddari, the reed-cutters, for their work, so that boats could sail even in the shallowest water without ever running aground. These boats were known as quarare and there is only one left to remind us of these long-lost crafts. It has been set atop a large reef that rose near the bank and now, set on the green lawn, the quarara is the pedestal for a rare *Agave medio-picta alba* surrounded by white stones, acting as its pot.

Nearby, a young *Sabal* palm flaunts its large keeled leaves that look like the prow of a wide pirogue riding the waves and raising foamy clouds of water.

Near it is a *Colletia cruciata*, a strange Uruguayan plant with fleshy and perfectly geometrical leaves that look like dozens of little jet planes.

We then greet another *Graevillea robusta* that blossoms into saffron yellow, followed by a lovely *Brachychiton* with its red trumpet-shaped flowers.

The thorny trail

I would like to extend the trail even further and bring visitors along the path going south of the garden, along the fence.

This is a unique trail, because on the other side of the fence we have planted a series of *opuntiae* – all different – that form an incredible green barrier that is thorny but succulent, exuberant and impassable. There are impressive specimens of *Opuntia cilindrica*, *Nopalea dejecta* and *Opuntia Santa Rita*, set between tall columns of *Cereus spachianus* facing each other, and when they blossom they mingle their large, sensuous flowers with the little red and yellow ones of their other succulent sisters.
The garden slopes gently to the right, along the large green field that has been left as a meadow, with very few plants for a sweeping view, a place to enjoy the countryside near and far.
Two specimens of *Agave salmiana* that are about ten years old – twins – are in the middle of two paths that descend to embrace them, and this is where we will plant lovely rows of aromatic plants: blue rosemary, white rosemary, lavender, thyme, lemongrass, aromatic sage, myrtle, laurel, basil and peppermint, in a blend of Mediterranean perfumes that give so much flavour to our cuisine.
I still have so many dreams in mind at my venerable old age. When you create a garden, you never stop making plans for it – just as you would with a child. When we built a fence around it in 1991, I had the impression that, at least, I had delimited it. And yet just beyond the fence we planted all those little palms, like you see in a nursery, and now they look at us and ask, 'What is our role in this garden?'.
I have plans for them, but for the time being they are only in my heart and mind, and I don't know if I'll live long enough to carry them out. I would like to try, but for now they're ideas and they must still materialise.
My other aspiration is water – again, in memory of the lake.

We take the road to the north, along the border. This was created with a beautiful row of elms, but the terrible disease that destroyed all the specimens in Europe, and that arrived here later, is now killing them one by one.
For now, it is an atypical road of *Yucca elephantipes* alternating with *Agave americane marginate*, with a lovely grove of *Pinus alepensis* along one side. On the other side, we may plant a row of *Phoenix canariensis*, which we have already potted so they won't run the risk of disease.

The end of the tour
We're back to where we started our tour and the visit is over. I couldn't mention all the plants, all the succulents, all the bushes. Each has its own place and its own space.
The gate opens again and my visitors leave, forever remembering that feeling of peace and mystery that is in the air here, amidst these rocks, and that makes our beloved garden so unique.

I want to tell you the story of some of our plants: how we discovered them, where we found and picked them, what they look like and their position today in the garden.
You'll find passages from the letters sent to us by our visitors, who have fully perceived all the passion, effort and love concealed in these branches, this space, these stones.
At the end of the book, there is also an index of all the species that are present here, to avoid offending any of our plant friends, so sensitive to the attention and love of those who tend them.

List of the garden plants

Acrotiche
Agavae: *ferox, medio-picta aurea, medio-picta alba, lophanta poselgeri, attenuata, salmiana, decipiens, americana albicans, americana marginata, colorata, ferdinandi regii, victoria regina, filifera, furcroides, latissima, noli tangere, potatorum, sisalana, americana striata*
Aloe
Bougainvillea
Carissa
Cipresses
Dasylirion longissimus
Enchephalartus horridus
Euphorbia canariensis
Grapefruits
Jasminus humilis
Opuntiae: *Nopalea dejecta, opunzia inermis, la robusta*
Pachipodium rosolatum
Parkinsonia aculeata
Schinus molle (falso pepe)
Terrace cactus
Xanthorrea arborea
Yucche: *elephantypes, gloriosa, aloifolia, marginata, rupicola*

Agave ferox
Family: amarillydaceae
Origin: Mexico

On Montecristo, a marvellous island off the Argentario coast in Tuscany, there is a house known as 'the King's house', so called because Victor Emanuel III would go there to hunt the mouflons and partridges that were so plentiful on the wild and mountainous island. Today, it is a protected natural reserve and not even boats are allowed to moor there.
Scipione and I went there about twenty years ago to swim in that heavenly clear blue water.
Near the guardhouse and all around 'the King's house', there were many large succulents that caught our attention, as we were already seeking new plants to bring back to Case del Biviere.
The guardian's kind wife gave us a shoot from a splendid *Agave ferox*, a precious treasure wrapped in newspaper that had to wait many days before being bedded in Sicily.
Now we have numerous plants dotting the garden, but the most spectacular is the one at the bottom of the two stairs going down to the pool. Its is perfectly shaped, and its wide, thick, tough dark-green leaves are topped by long, thick, sharp, black spines, whilst hooked spines of various sizes are spaced along the edges of the leaves
It is set at a slant, facing west as if it wanted to bask in the very last rays of sunshine.

E.S.

Agave Victoria Regina
Family: amaryllidaceæ
Origin: Central America, Mexico

This is a small agave, but it is truly a rare and special plant. It was tiny when we bought it from a nursery near Catania back in 1967. It was the first plant to arrive at Case del Biviere, and because of this I am very fond of it.

It was bedded on the east jetty and, today, it cuts a fine figure alongside another small and extraordinary agave, the *Ferdinandi regii*. It looks like a large succulent rose, deep green in colour. Each of its wide, fleshy, carinate leaves is edged with a thin chalky line, almost as if a skilful painter had decided to let his imagination run wild to create a showy plant. Its apical spines are stiff and dangerous.

Like all agaves, it blossoms just once in its lifetime and then dies. As opposed to its sisters, however, it does not generate any basal shoots: it reproduces only through the bulbils from its inflorescences. This makes it extremely rare and quite long-lived: it can supposedly live up to fifty years.

The word 'agave' comes from the Greek *agauos*, meaning 'marvellous', and all of its countless existing specimens are marvellous indeed.

E.S

Aloe saponaria
Family: liliaceæ
Origin: South Africa

This is a succulent that looks somewhat like an agave, but it does not belong to the same family and the only thing reminiscent of the agave is its rosette shape, with thick leaves dotted with spines.
There are countless species – acaulous and with trunks, solitary or in groups, striated, spotted, spiny, hanging and ribbon-like.
The one we're talking about here arrived in our garden in the Seventies from Palermo, and we were able to use shoots to reproduce quite a large number. We even dedicated a big and charming flowerbed to them, on the slope separating the upper part of the garden from the swimming pool area.
We planted them next to each other so they are touching. All these speckled moss-green plants are about the same size, and they are crowned with little orangey spines. The highlight comes when they blossom, and they are simultaneously covered with long stems with delightful pinkish-orange bell-shaped flowers. I can assure you that it is a fascinating sight!
The aborigines would use the gelatine that oozes from the cut leaves to treat wounds and to wash their hands when they were particularly dirty – hence the name 'soap aloe'.

E.L

Cephalocereus polylophus
Family: cactaceæ (*Neubuxbaumia*)
Origin: Mexico

We bought it from the Sciacca nursery in December 1980, and for many years it was in a terracotta pot near the stairs leading down to the garden. It never bloomed, but when it got too big to live in that vase, we transplanted it to the large terrace across from the grapefruit trees, along the front of the house in one of the four stone-enclosed flowerbeds, each of which has a different cactacea. Now it flowers every year, in July and August, with an abundance of striking ruby-red flowers that form marvellous coloured crowns around the large green trunk, which was 2.5 metres tall by the summer of 2001. It has closely set ribs and its spines are a lovely golden yellow.

E.S.

Cereus Iamacaru
Family: cactaceæ
English name: The queen of the night
Origin: Brazil

The first small specimen arrived in Biviere in 1970 from the garden of Terre Rosse in Palermo and we potted it. Then a few years later, we planted it in the ground to the left of the swimming pool because of its beautiful night blooming in mid-summer that makes it so intriguing and sensuous. Today, it is enormous, its numerous branches stretching up to the sky. At its feet, I planted a jasmine that surrounds the plant with its scent. Its blossom lasts just one night, opening at dusk and dropping to the ground, closed, the next morning. Scipione took several cuttings and there is now a large plant under the west window of the dining room, set between two ramparts – a spectacular giant.

E.S.

Chorisia speciosa
Family: bombacaceæ
Origin: Brazil, Argentina

In January of 1981, at a nursery near Catania we bought a little plant in a pot that looked a bit sickly and had four little leaves on a spiny trunk.
I have always worked with my imagination, and so even before I transplanted it I could picture luxuriant flowering foliage and a curved trunk, like so many of the ones I had seen in Palermo and Catania.
We had to wait a long time before it reached a substantial size, but now – in October 2001 – our *Chorisia* has regaled us with countless fuchsia blossoms, enormous flowers that resemble orchids. They last just one day before they drop to the foot of the trunk, creating a rosy halo on the lawn.
Today, its greenish trunk is thick and sturdy, with short, round, strong spines and an utterly unique appearance. Its roots rise from the soil like a family of slinking snakes. During the short spring and in the summer, it is covered with large greenish pods that are about ten centimetres long. When they are ripe, they open to release large balls of silky white floss that flutters across the lawn. Inside, there are hundreds of large black seeds. This year, I gathered about 700 and at different times of the year, I am planting them in small pots in order to reproduce these plants.
In its country of origin, the plant is known as *Palo borracho*, because it resembles a bottle.
It was named in honour of the botanist J. L. Choris.

E.S.

Citrus Paradisi (grapefruit)
Family: rutaceæ
Origin: Far East

In 1985, we decided to decorate the main entrance to the house. There is a terrace in front of it, set on a bed of tufaceous rock that sustains all the buildings. We planted four lovely specimens of Citrus paradisi, better known as grapefruit, of the 'Marsh seedless' variety, distinguished its lovely golden pulp.
We chose them in honour of Sicily, which was famous by then as the land of oranges. What better way to make a wonderful first impression on our visitors than these glossy, luxuriant trees, with golden fruit peeking from their branches almost all year round, so appetising, precious and inviting?
As the story goes, the fruit of Paradise wasn't the pomegranate but Citrus paradisi, and in this mythical land that emanates legend and serenity, this is what we like to believe.
We have planted them in four large beds, carved out on the ground floor and outlined with lovely rectangular stones, with round white rocks scattered around the trunks. What a delightfully cheerful sight!
And let's not forget its scent, which explodes suddenly and intensely on April nights when the trees are covered with showy citrus blossoms. Their fragrance is overwhelming and as it surrounds us, it evokes memories of extraordinary Oriental evenings.

E.S.

Dasylirion hookeri
Family: liliaceæ
Origin: Southern U.S., Mexico

In 1988, at a nursery near Catania, off in the corner we saw a pot with a healthy tuft of long, slender leaves that opened up in an arch, like fireworks about to explode.
We brought it home and the next day, we decided to give it a special place, so that everyone coming through the main gate could admire it. And so, with the utmost care and attention, after preparing a large and well-drained hole and filling it with soil mixed with sand and gravel, we placed it to the right of the entry to chapel of St. Andrew, near the stone corner that frames it so elegantly. A few feet away from it is one of the two eighteenth-century benches – slightly crooked but lovely nevertheless – that beckon one to stop and meditate.
It has grown there, slowly but vigorously, and it has turned into a splendid and showy specimen. When it is illuminated at night, it truly looks like a firework display.
This year, 2001, it has sprouted a long inflorescence, an arm outstretched toward the sky. Day after day, it has become taller and more impressive, reaching a height of nearly four metres. In June, it turned a deep brick red, leaving our visitors speechless!
In September, when its stunning colour was gone and tiny seeds appeared, we covered it with a sheet of non-woven fabric, which we tied at the base of the flowers so we could collect and sow the seeds – although I know that they will not germinate easily.

ES

Dracaena draco
Family: liliaceæ
Origin: Canary Islands

Every botanical garden and all the loveliest public and private gardens in Sicily have a spectacular *Dracaena draco*, which is marked by its numerous branches and inflorescences. In the garden of Case del Biviere, there is only one specimen and it dates to 1990, the year it was bedded near a small stone arch separating the area of the *Phoenix canariensis* from the large covered area we use for dinners and receptions.

It has a lovely pale and sturdy trunk with just one head, composed of ensiform leaves set in a rosette. We were afraid it wouldn't do well, because in winter the temperature can even drop below zero, whereas this species need constant warmth. The wall to the north certainly protects it, but it was a big risk. The plant apparently liked us, because during these eleven years of growth it began to blossom and then branch out, until reaching a very dignified shape and size.

Its name comes from the Greek *drakaina*, or 'female dragon'. Its sap is reddish and gummy, and can be used as sealing wax. In the past, it was also used as a miraculous medicine. The Dracaena draco is said to live for a thousand years, but since we can't calculated its age by counting the circles of its trunk – it is a spongy plant – we must rely on legend.

Euphorbia grandidens
Family: euphorbiaceæ
Origin: Madagascar

It is named after Euphorbus, the physician of the King of Numidia and Mauritania, who dedicated the plant to his doctor because of its therapeutic properties.
The genus includes a very large number of species that differ greatly in shape, colour and size. The one trait they share is the whitish latex that oozes from their branches or leaves when they are broken in half. This liquid is very irritating and in the *grandidens*, it is especially poisonous and harmful to the eyes.
We have a number of different specimens, but we have planted the most spectacular one to the right of the stairs that, on the western side of the house, lead down to the garden. It is set against a low wrought-iron railing, with a large *Yucca elephantipes*, a fragrant *Stephanotis* and a new arrival, a *Pereskia aculeata*, as its neighbours. Nearby, there is also a lovely *Cereus Jamacaru*, as well as the light blue and white leadworts that adorn our little 'boutique'. It is an ensemble that is very green and tropical, but also fragrant and colourful, making the little corner near the living room doorway quite charming.
It arrived in our garden about twelve years ago, a small green cutting given to us by a nursery. It initially took in a pot and after it was bedded, it unleashed all its vigour. It looks like a powerful column with long curved branches spewing from it in disarray, like the Medusa's head.

Myrtillocactus geometrizans
Family: cactaceæ
English name: Blue myrtle
Origin: Mexico

It has been on the east jetty for years and was one of the first little plants we bedded, a gift from Monica and Elisabeth when they returned from one of their outings in the area. It is a lovely cerulean green, with spines that are spaced widely apart in an even pattern. It has many branches and its lignescent trunk changes colour. It suffers the cold but bears up, undaunted! I am very attached to it.

Opuntia Santa Rita
Family: cactaceæ
Origin: Southeast Arizona

It arrived in our garden many years ago, in the Eighties I think, and it was just a little cutting with a few spiny and perfectly round leaves. We bedded it on the west jetty and, as happens with almost every new arrival we plant, we didn't take its future size into account. Slowly but surely, year after year our plant grew and today it is a large and very spiny bush in the middle of the jetty.
What makes it so unique is its spectacular flowering. In the beginning of May, it is covered with hundreds of buds with a rosy-coloured tip, and then exactly on the 26th of May, the feast of St. Rita of Cascia, the buds blossom into a myriad of bright yellow flowers that are so shiny they almost look as if they have been lacquered. They don't last long, but in a garden you must learn to enjoy these 'magical moments', brief as they may be, that Mother Nature suddenly bestows on us.

E.S.

Orocereus celsianus
Family: cactaceæ
English name: The old man of the Andes
Origin: Peruvian, Bolivian and Chilean Andes

In January of 1980 I went to a nursery set between the bends leading to Ragusa Ibla and off in a corner, I noticed a cactus that was a little over 30 centimetres tall, covered with coarse whitish hair. I immediately took a shine to it. I bought it and the next day, I transplanted it to a larger terracotta vase. To make it look even more important, I then placed it in a splendid eighteenth-century vase from Caltagirone with a light background and vertical light-blue and orange stripes. I put it to the left of the stairs going down to the pool and for a few years, out of fear that it would be too cold in the winter and too hot in the summer, I planted a little umbrella next to it that protected it from the weather but made it look a little ridiculous. It became perfectly acclimated and now, twenty years later, it is 1.70 metres tall and has sprouted two splendid daughters with thick hair.

Pachipodium giganteum
Family: apocynaceæ
Origin: Southwest Africa

I received many specimens as gifts, but they didn't thrive. Some died of the cold, others from funguses, and others due to mysterious circumstances.
Scipione and I refused to give up, because this plant is quite beautiful and highly decorative.
Finally, in 1995 we went to the Valentino nursery near Ragusa and purchased a stunning specimen that had already branched and thus had two heads. We decided to put it against the wall of the main house. We planted it in one of the five large flowerbeds aligned against the façade and edged with lovely tufaceous rocks, with round white stones at the base that contrasted with the cerulean blue of the plant's large and flask-shaped aculeate trunk.
Not only did our newest arrival like its position, but apparently it also enjoyed the company of other cactaceae, each of which was planted in a different flowerbed – all in a row like armed green warriors.
In June of 2000 and of 2001, our *Pachipodium* bloomed with marvellous white flowers that closely resemble those of both the oleander (from the same family) and the plumeria or frangipani. It blossoms on new branches that form specifically to generate clusters of apical flowers. Now there are six branches, which will probably double next year.
Its name is derived from the Greek *pachìs podòs*, meaning large foot.

Parkinsonia aculeata
Family: leguminosæ
Origin: Tropical America, Island of Cape Verde

I went to Greece in July of 1980. It was a long hot summer and I can still remember the scents and colours of the Peloponnesian islands. We arrived at the island of Simi and the bell tower of its white monastery, set in the middle of the long low building, is so dazzlingly white against the sapphire sea that you can see it from far off in the distance.

We were welcomed by a certain Pope with a long grizzled beard, eyes as light as the water of the Greek sea, and a sweet and gentle smile. He took us on a tour of the church, aglitter with gold and burning candles, and then he led us to a charming patio with two trees that I thought were quite extraordinary. Their slender leaves were as light and feathery as pine needles, and in the middle were the last yellow flowers, stained with red, in dense clusters that smelled like jasmine. The luxuriant branches and part of the trunk were a silken emerald green, studded with treacherous little spines. The seeds, enclosed in little tobacco-coloured pods, were already ripe so I asked if I could take one. The man agreed, and only someone who has created a garden little by little can understand the joy you feel when you discover a plant you've never seen before.

That autumn, we put the seeds in pots protected from the cold and the following spring I already had a lovely little seedling, ready to be transplanted. It is named after Mr. Parkinson, a botanical artist for the British Empire who accompanied Captain Cook during one of his trips to the Orient. His assignment was to sketch all the exotic plants he found and bring the seeds back to England. Unfortunately, Mr. Parkinson died on the journey home and thus the little plants that arrived in England were named *Parkinsonia aculeata* in his honour. Now my little plant is a large and thriving tree with long feathery foliage, and in June it is covered with flowers that give off an intense perfume.

When she visited my garden in June of 1988, Elizabeth, the Queen Mother, fell in love with the *Parkinsonia* and was delighted one Christmas when I sent her a lovely specimen that is now in the royal greenhouse at Kew Gardens.

Phytolacca dioica
Family: phytolaccaceæ
Argentine names: Bela sombra or Ombu
Origin: Argentina

In the summer of 1986, we went to Monteargentario, where we were the guests of Alberto Milla at Cala Grande. The house – cool and welcoming – is set in the middle of the Maremma underbrush and the pine and ilex forests, and it is surrounded by rare plants from around the world. Among them are marvellous specimens of Phytolacca dioica, with thick fleshy roots rising from the soil, almost like hippopotamuses surfacing from the swamp water.

These plants have lovely bright green foliage, with evident veins and broad, beckoning leaves. Its name comes from Greek and means 'dye plant', as its fruit yields scarlet juice that is used to colour wines and sweets.

One of the oddities about this plant is that, apparently, no one has ever seen it die or catch fire – and it is never attacked by animal parasites.

Our host allowed us to take two cuttings. Our daughter Monica planted them in pots on her terrace in Rome, and then she brought one to Biviere. Today, her tiny garden near Corso Francia has a large specimen that is thriving, whilst the one in Biviere is now a lovely, luxuriant and dramatic tree.

Rosa fortuniana
Family: rosaceæ
Origin: China

When we arrived in Biviere, on the western side near one of the old ramparts made of tuff blocks sustaining the houses, there was a small and thirsty rosebush with just one white bud on its branches. I knew nothing about its name or origin, and I decided to transplant it in a pot so that I could plant it later in a better spot. It quickly grew into a luxuriant bush that was covered with little white rosebuds by the middle of April.
I decided to take some cuttings and Scipione, who was always in charge of this kind of work, prepared several different specimens. In just a few years, the number of plants multiplied.
We planted one in the ground to the left of the chapel of St. Andrew, another one at the corner near the inn, and the third one directly in front of the white oleander, which flowers during a completely different period than the rosebush.
Within a few years, the three bushes – two of which face each other – became big green islands that, in April, are covered with snow-white pompons set all in a row along the hanging branches.
During a guided tour, a group of English botanists was enchanted by the dazzling blossoms on one of my rosebushes, observing its leaves, its few thorns and the position of the flowers. When they left, they took some small branches and a few rosebuds with them. A few months later, I received a letter with a photograph – and the news that my rosebush had been discovered in China by a Mr. Fortune. It is a *Banxia* that is suited only for the Mediterranean climate. It was named after its discoverer and is thus known as *Rosa fortuniana*. I was pleased and delighted, for I thought this name was a good omen.

Xanthorrea arborea
Family: liliaceæ
English name: Blackboy
Origin: Australia

In June of 1978, Scipione and I were near Ragusa and as we passed a beautiful farm that had partly fallen into ruin, we saw some workmen struggling to remove a strange plant with a wrinkled trunk and ruffled foliage with long, slender, sharp leaves. The plant was in flower – a single inflorescence that was over three metres long. Intrigued, we stopped to ask what they were planning to do with it and they said they were trying to uproot it completely because they had to repair the wall next to it, which had nearly collapsed under the weight of the plant. The very same thought came into our heads, and Scipione and I asked the men if we could arrange to remove it ourselves and take it with us. They immediately agreed, delighted that they had found an easy solution to their problem. The following day, a small lorry brought the plant to Biviere. It looked enormous with its quivering plume, and I could picture it at the corner of the main façade, facing southeast. Planting it upright was quite difficult because the head was so heavy. There was a strong risk that it would fall over with wind or rain, so I decided to plant it in a recumbent position, with its roots at the corner of the house, held down by a massive piece of basalt, and its long trunk lying on the ground. Its head, lying on a large tufaceous rock, gives it the appearance of a lady at rest, a green Paulina welcoming visitors with great dignity. We have identified it in our books: it is a *Xanthorrea arborea*, a plant originally from Australia and member of the liliaceae family. It blossoms only once every ten years. Its genus is *Dasylirion* and after it flowers, the number of heads doubles. Now it is an extraordinary specimen with six impressive and ruffled heads – a green monument.

E.S.

Washingtonia robusta
Family: palmæ
Origin: California

In 1978, our friend Umbertina came to lunch one day and brought us a long narrow terracotta pot, which I still have. Inside was a small palm tree with just two leaves. It was a small *Washingtonia robusta* from her charming little garden in the heart of Ortigia, in Siracusa.
We planted it very carefully in the area near the pool, setting up a small fence around it so no one would step on it!
Now it is about 25 metres tall and it looms over all the other trees around it. Over the years, it has generated many little palms, both individuals and groups, many of which have been transplanted. Four splendid groups of three, four and even five specimens each were placed near the swimming pool in 1984 and they are truly spectacular.

Yucca elephantipes
Family: liliaceæ
Origin: Mexico, Guatemala

The first little plants arrived from Palermo in 1969 and were planted in the little port that had just been filled with clayey soil, near the two long, stone jetties that somehow managed to protect them from the cold and the north wind.
Today, they are colossal plants with powerful and wrinkly greyish bases that look amazingly like elephants' feet. Their bright green leaves are lanceolate and sharp. All summer long and well into the autumn, the tips of their branches sprout tall inflorescences, composed of clusters of little white bells that flutter in the wind.
These plants are extremely dramatic because of their power and size, and they can easily be compared with mighty living statues. All the plants in this species have found their ideal habitat at Case del Biviere: they flourish and reproduce very easily from cuttings we take from their woody branches.
The irrigation system in the garden makes them even more splendid and colourful. They do not suffer from funguses and they are not attacked by animal parasites.

Appendix

Garden's guests
(a few extracts of letters sent to Miki and Scipione Borghese)

20-5-1987

[...] tutti i rallegramenti per il gioiello del giardino creato dal niente con tanta passione e competenza.
È veramente straordinario il lavoro svolto per ottenere in pochi anni un risultato così sorprendente che certamente ripaga tanta abnegazione. Ne siamo rimasti tutti incantati

Marisa Sgaravatti
Presidente Società Amici del Giardinaggio,
Padova

20 giugno 1988

Carissima Signora Michi,
[...] È un piccolo pensiero per dirle ancora grazie e per farvi i complimenti per come avete saputo sistemare con eleganza il giardino. [...]

Niccolò Grassi, Milano

16 dicembre 1988

Gentili amici,
ricordo quel giorno delle breve sosta nella Vostra casa tanto ospitale di Biviere, una settimana fa, come in un sogno che ha attraversato giornate ben diverse, di corse e di lavoro. È rimasta tuttavia in me un'ammirazione profonda e sincera. [...]

Giuliano Vassalli, Roma

1° maggio 1989

Gentilissima Principessa,
Il suo giardino – ricco di colori e piante grasse – resta uno dei più bei ricordi del viaggio Garden-Sicilia 1989.

Gabriella Bernardini,
consigliere Garden Club Verona

2 maggio 1989

Gentile Signora,
[...] voglia gradire i più entusiastici ed ammirati complimenti al raro equilibrio del Suo parco ma soprattutto alla brillante asciuttezza della Sua personalità dalla quale il parco è sicuramente nato. [...]

Marisa Zenari
Garden Club Verona

20 maggio 1989

Ho ancora presente e vivo nell'animo, gentile Amica, il ricordo del suo affascinante paradiso mediterraneo, la gamma di verdi e di fiori, la cortesia dei padroni di casa; un tutto che ha rappresentato per noi veronesi l'ospitalità di una terra appena riscoperta e subito amata.
Grazie per averci accolte con tanta affabilità e per averci iniziate alla conoscenza di una flora variegatissima e ricca di seduzioni.
Sentivo di doverle personalmente il mio grazie, non disgiunto da una certa nostalgia, ma anche un arrivederci nel Nord, che mi auguro vicino.
A presto, dunque, con un verde fascio di auguri da

Mina Veronese de Poli, Verona

3 January 1991

[...] My husband says he learnt so much about your trees he was delighted. And I found the juxtaposition of shapes and forms and textures amongst the bushes and trees you did with such artistry. [...]

Rachel Holtam, Dorchester, Dorset

9 October 1991

[…] We saw many magnificant things in our two weeks abroad, but nothing was more moving than the masterpiece in time and space that you have created, and no one was more exciting and angaging than you. […]

Susan J. Barnes
Senior Curator of Western Art
Dallas Museum of Art

Clarence House, January 4th 1992

Dear Princess Borghese,
It is so very kind of you to give me the beautiful Parkinsonia aculeata and I am thrilled to have this glorious tree. It is now under glass, and I am just hoping that it will be happy in the garden, when Summer comes.
I remember with such pleasure my visit to your lovely and interesting garden. With renewed thanks to you both, I am ever yours sincerely

Elisabeth R

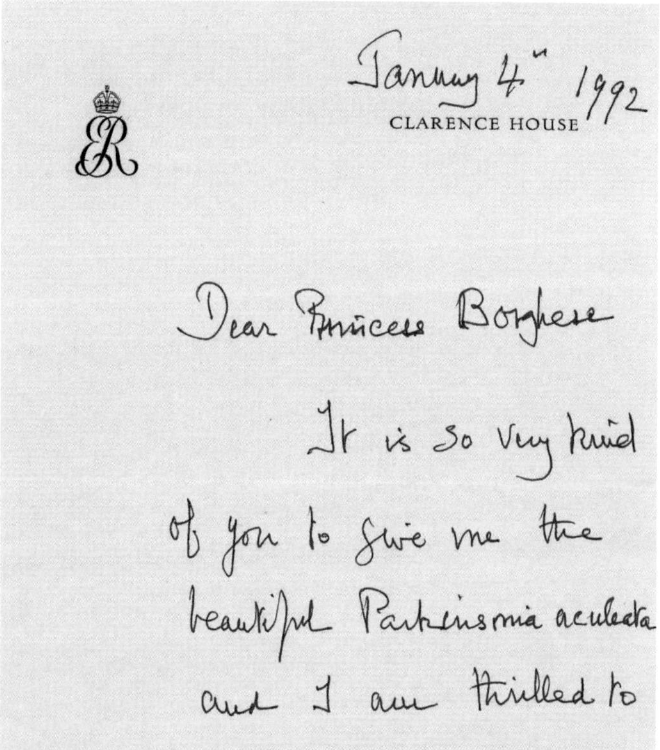

January 4th 1992

CLARENCE HOUSE

Dear Princess Borghese

It is so very kind of you to give me the beautiful Parkinsonia aculeata and I am thrilled to have this glorious tree. It is now under glass, and I am just hoping

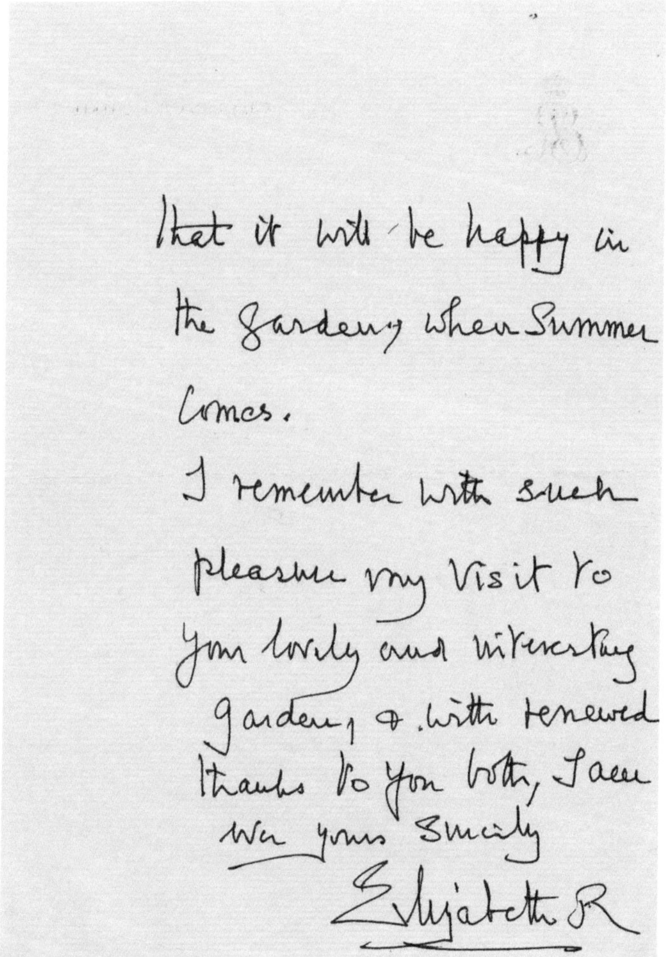
that it will be happy in the gardens when Summer comes.

I remember with such pleasure my visit to your lovely and interesting garden, & with renewed thanks to you both, I am ever yours sincerely

Elizabeth R

Ottobre 1992

Principessa,
[...] è stata per me una vera emozione visitare il suo giardino: le esprimo tutta la mia ammirazione per questa sua opera che si vede fatta con grande arte e vera partecipazione. [...]

Federico Milesi, Milano

7 November 1992

[...] I don't think I've ever seen a garden lovelier than yours, and I'm certain I've never seen one privately owned with such an incredible variety of uniquely wonderful trees and shrubs. The more I think about them, remember, the more I marvel at the way you and your husband have been able to incorporate such diverse elements into such a harmonious and elegant whole. [...]

Nancy S. Ross

October 4th, 1993

Dear Principessa,
I am very glad that we saved up your garden for the final visit on the tour. All the garden enthusiasts werw ecstatic, and Robin Lane Fox equates your garden with Ninfa, which is praise indeed. [...]

Charles FitzRoy, London

18-3-1994

[...] You gave us a fascinating afternoon and I came away amazed and impressed by your energy and creative vision in the making of a truly magical garden. I do hope you will tell the story of the house, the lake and its extraordinary transformation as I think it both a fascinating story and a wonderful subject for an illustrated book. [...]

Peter Lauritzen, Venezia

9 giugno 1994

È stato un incontro meraviglioso, interessante in un giardino incantato e di rara bellezza [...]

Floriana Mentasti Granelli

10-10-1994

[...] It was wonderful for us to see a garden conceived wuth such originality and imagination combined with such horticultural expertise and faultless good taste. It was a sane treat for us to see such a place so unique in its situation and realization. [...] They have used a long-abandoned harbour with its wharves, walls and associated buildings as a unique setting in which to grow an extraordinary range of plants. [...]
Il Biviere's three-a-half hectare garden is not only a remarkable horticultural achievemnet but it changes our view of the way in which a succulent garden can be made.

Patrick Bowe
Architect and Garden Designer, Dublin

27 novembre 1994

[...] We were both fascinated by the idea – and the story of – the garden planted in the old lakebed and we were delighted by the result which enabled us to enjoy a splendid lunch in such a marvellous setting. [...]

Trevor and Anne Wayne, Falconwood

28 maggio 1995

[...] your garden magnificent. I still can't imagine it was once a harbor. You should certainly proceed with your book. [...]

Victoria Rothschild

10 ottobre 1995

Gentile Signora,
veramente senza difficoltà – forse perché smorzata da certa persistente tenerezza, dopo l'incantevole vissuta realtà – ho ritrovato il "biviere" accen-

nato da Salvatore Quasimodo nella sua poesia: "al padre". È una delle più importanti cose da lui scritte nella seconda metà degli anni cinquanta in raccolta poi dedicata a "la terra impareggiabile" pubblicata nell'estate del 1958.
Questa raccolta comprende anche la poesia: "un'anfora di rame" che ora sento più compiutamente perché:
"Le spine dei fichidindia
"sulla siepe.......
"..forse a Lentini vicino la palude
"di Jacopo notaio.....

non sono più per me un paesaggio di sogno.

Walter Galli, Milano

[attached]
"[...] Le spine dei fichidindia/sulla siepe, il tuo corpetto strappato/appena azzurro e nuovo, un dolore/al centro del cuore scavato,/forse a Lentini vicino la palude/di Iacopo notaio d'anguille/e d'amori" [...].
(Salvatore Quasimodo, *Un'anfora di rame*)
"[...] E ora nell'aquila dei tuoi novant'anni/ho voluto parlare con te, coi tuoi segnali/di partenza colorati dalla lanterna/notturna, e qui da una ruota/imperfetta del mondo,/su una piena di muri serrati,/lontano dai gelsomini d'Arabia/dove ancora tu sei, per dirti/ciò che non potevo un tempo – difficile affinità/di pensieri – per dirti, e non ci ascoltano solo/cicale del biviere, agavi lentischi,/come il campiere dice al suo padrone:/«Baciamu li mani». Questo, non altro./Oscuramente forte è la vita".
(Salvatore Quasimodo, *Al padre*)

4 giugno 1996

Il venire al Biviere è stata un'esperienza così immensamente dolce: il colore dei fiori, il tenero verde dei prati, le piante, tutte insieme condite dalla loro squisita accoglienza, come dicevo a sua figlia sono quelle cose che uno chiude nel cuore a consolazione di tempi peggiori.
Dappertutto si sentiva il Loro amore per il bello della natura e il lavoro continuo ed appassionato che ci sta dietro.

Marco Matteucci, Merano

8 giugno 1996

[...] nel suo meraviglioso giardino mediterraneo.
È stata un'esperienza unica e il fatto che lei e suo marito, con tanto coraggio ed entusiasmo, abbiate trasformato in attrazione una terra arida, mi fa sperare con più forza di prima negli uomini. [...]

Barbara e Luigi Novicelli

Financial Times, 26 October 1996

Marshland to green oasis
Robin Lane Fox admires a garden in Sicily that has adapted to its harsh surroundings

The gardens in Britain are on the turn and the bleakness of winter is beginning to beckon. Garden vistas can be desolate in colder climates, but I am comforting myself with memories of a recent visit to a once desolate site, now a green oasis of a garden in the Mediterranean.
The eastern coast of Sicily has many times been a friendly paradise to settlers. The first Greek settlers in the age of Homer chose to found cities along its coastline. The mystical hero Heracles was said to have worked all sorts of wonders in the landscape, though some of them are hard to see nowadays between the *zona industriale* and the motorways.
Near the ancient Greek site of Leontini, there is still a trace of one of Heracles' miracles. Heracle was said to have laid out a marvellous lake, teeming with wildlife. No doubt it delighted the early Greeks and, until the 1930s, it delighted the sporting Sicilians who used it for their favourite sport of duck shooting.
The lake, however, began to teem with malaria and in the interests of public health had to be drained. The water vanished and the hinterland of ancient Leontini was left with a bare, brown depression.
The area around the lake forms part of the ancestral estates of the Borghese family and in the late 1960s, a Roman Borghese brought his young bride, Princess Scipione, back to live on the Sicilian property.
Lesser women would have bolted to Portofino at the first glimpse of their future prospective. Princess Scipione stayed, however, and, since 1968,

has joined her husband in creating Italy's only newly planted private garden. The result deserves international respect.
The former marshland at Casa del Biviere is surrounded by mature trees which are familiar to botanical connoisseurs but will surprise visitors on the botanical trail. I have seen the garden twice and I can only admire the determination, artistry and perseverance that have given rise to such an unusual style. It is a living example of garden-making in adversity, with lessons for anyone who believes that their land is too forlorn for gardening to be a serious possibility.
Eastern Sicily is ferociously hot in summer and anyone considering gardening then as an immediate problem with water.
Heracles' lake may have seeped deeper than one would care to drill with boreholes, but this has not deterred the Borgheses. In September, the garden is still green, beautifully settled, with ingeniously chosen evergreens and plants which can store sufficient water for the hot season.
The garden illustrates how to use and choose plants, such as the giant Yuccas and Agaves, in climates where the temperature soars and retricts choice.
Superb specimen of yucca Rupicola and huge agave Ferox have developed beside the garden's handsome steps and terraces, contrasting dramatically with the staircases of strong stone blocks and the walls of the country house.
At Biviere, the Organ Cacti rise to 20ft or more as a magnificent vertical line, while a stupendous Furcea carries no less than eight flowers, like the tails of an enormous, grassy animal, one of the only flowering specimens to be seen in Italy.
Beside a Sicilian country house, cacti and yuccas present a most unexpected focus for a formal garden plan and are architectural masterpieces in their own right.
You might expect blue-flowering plumbago in a good Italian garden, but you are unlikely to meet a bigger or more effective groups than the sky-blue plumbagos beside the family chapel.
You might also expect the occasional citrus tree, but you would not be prepared for a splendid, glossy green hedge of grapefruits along the garden's lower level.
The trees look as if they has arrived long before 1968 and anyone would covet the blue-flowered Jacarandas which have developed beside the jetty of Heracles' former lake.

There is a magnificient airy specimen of Parkinsonia aculeata with its light leaves and red and yellow flowers. The prickly trunks of Corresias, as well as the native Agnus casti, add variety to plantings which might otherwise be nothing but a contrast of spikes and feathers.
I was most surprised by the roses. I am never sure whether they will flourish in very hot gardens and frost-free climates. At Biviere, Britains familiar whiteflowered rose Alberic barbier is in excellent health and accompanied by the pink rose Clare Martin.
The Borgheses have been careful to collect some of the wild roses to be found on nearby Mount Etna and surrounding hills. The small-leaved rose Fortuneiana even puzzled a visiting party from the Royal Horticultural Society, but eventually it was identified and confirmed by specimens of its white flowers.
The Borghese garden is an object lesson in how to surmount adversity and not to reject a bleak horizon that is seemingly empty of any single living object of friendliness or distinction.
There is now a green haven with a canopy of mature trees, persuading the visitor that nature briefly relented and decided to make up for the surrounding bleakness by allowing a garden of 5 acres to flourish.
Visits to Leontini may not be on everyone's itinerary and unfortunately the Borghese garden is not open to the public, partly because there is no demand locally.

1 novembre 1996

Princesse,
Cette visite à Biviere à été un enchantement [...]
Je suis remplie d'admiration en pensant à toute la perseverence et à toute l'imagination que vous avez du déployer pour la création de ce superbe jardin.

Jeanne Marie Hennesy

1 November 1996

[...] It was a particular pleasure to see how cleverly you had created such a beautiful garden under such difficult conditions. [...]

Barbara Keeve

12 febbraio 1997

Gentile amica,
non sarà facile dimenticare la nostra visita al "Biviere": siamo stati conquistati dalla atmosfera che vi regnava, da tanti spunti insoliti e suggestivi.
La sua arguta presentazione in cappella, il suo giardino dove le aloi e le agavi fanno da padrone, il vecchio imbarcadero, i tronchi gemmati degli alberi, la squisitezza del cibo servito, e soprattutto la simpatia dei padroni di casa rimarranno, le assicuro, nel nostro cuore. [...]

Vittorio Santagostino
Presidente Società Orticola di Lombardia

Marzo 1997

[...] Il "Biviere" rimane nella memoria, vivido e preciso[...]

Battista Rispoli, Napoli

1-9-1997

Gentile signora Borghese,
al termine del nostro piacevolissimo viaggio in Sicilia, le scrivo per ringraziarla della bellissima occasione che mi ha offerto con la visita al suo giardino, una delle cose più belle che abbia visto in questa pur bellissima isola.
Forse di persona non le ho saputo manifestare quanto sia rimasta colpita, al di là della bellezza e della preziosità di ogni singola pianta, dall'equilibrio e dall'amore che spirano da questa sua creatura. [...]

Elena Manzoni, Como

1 March 1998

[...] the "succulent" garden is so unique! I especially like all green gardens. I am an architectural designer, so the elegant simplicity of your villa was so appealing, and definitely suits my American sensibility. [...]

Melvin Dwork

1 March 1998

[…] But, words escape me when I remember the beautiful gardens you have created. You are an inspiration to all of us who aspire to being gardeners! […]

Elinor K. Farquhar,
Washington, D.C.

March 28, 1998

[…] Your account of the garden was fascinating and helped us all appreciate the beauty of the landscape, trees, and plants and the difficulty of finding the right species of succulents and flowers. You have created an oasis in a challenging climate and terrain. […]

Michael Curchman
The Nelson-Atkins Museum of Art,
Kansas City, Missouri

April 23, 1998

[…] Robin Lane Fox was quite right when he described your Garden as the best in Italy – it was certainly our favourite. […]

Louise Allen
Deputy Superintendent,
The University of Oxford Botanic Garden

9 July 1998

[…] I was absolutely enchanted by the unique beauty of the garden you have so lovingly created. […]

Jeffrey Neal Blanchard, Rome

30 October 1998

Dear Principessa,
My husband and I much enjoyed writing your fascinating garden it is so different from any garden we could see here. We were able to appreciate your amazing collection of plants as we live near the Royal Botanical Gardens at Kew. [...]

Andrey Venty, Richmond, Surrey

4th October 1999

[...] I would never have dreamed that such a beautiful and unusual garden could exist so far south, and for us to find green lawns and plenty of dappled shade on one of the hottest days we could remember was a miracle! I so admired the positioning of your cacti, agave, succulents etc. They were all 'personalities' in their own right, but each one had just enough space to show itself off, and their different shapes complemented the plants to either side. One also felt that you had pur great thought into the views across the garden – so often through waving branches one caught a glimpse of a tall silhouette or a waving green sea of foliage caught in the breeze and these were unexpected bonuses. [...]

Mary Davie-Thornill, London

10th October 1999

[...] It was a great pleasure first to meet you and your charming husband and then to be shown around by you, so that you could explain to us, how this magical garden was created. It is truly extraordinary, quite unbelievable and must take you feel so proud. What a wonderful achievement. [...]

Violando Embiricos

16 mars 2000

[...] Nous avons été sé duits par la façon remarquable dont vous avez planté ces terres prises sur un lac asséché, pour en faire un parc plein de charme. [...]

Henry Racamier, Paris

28 October 2000

Dear Princess Borghese,
We have now returned to Menorca after our visit to Sicily of the meeting of the Mediterranean Garden Society in Palermo. Thank you so much for inviting us to your house and to see your beautiful garden. This was very much the highlight of our visit. It is particularly special to see a garden that has been created personally over a long period of time. [...]

Duncan Ackery,
Sant Lluis, Menorca

10-11-2000

[...] We were impressed by what you have achieved and delighted by the beauty you have created. The variety of plants, light and shade and the depth of yours garden were a work of art. [...]

Heidi Gildemeister
President, The Mediterranean Garden Society

20 November 2000

Dear Principessa,
One of the highlights of our most enjoyable visit to Sicily was luncheon at Il Biviere and the opportunity to see and admire your beautiful and unusual garden. We were full of admiration for what you have created – particularly the sense of peace and calm, in a setting which seemed to have been established for many, many more years than was in fact the case. We really did appreciate, and want to thank you for, your kindness in inviting us and entertaining us so well in such delightful and relaxed surroundings. [...]

Michael Hutchinson,
Guildford, Surrey

Dear Principessa Maria Carla,
[...] It was a great privilege, and a high light of our visit to Sicily, to see your beautiful house and garden. The garden was of great interest to us, and we thought your mixing of different shapes was especially artistic and a joy to see. I enjoyed seeing my fellow country man, the black boy, propped on his elbow.
We had a wonderful trip and gained much from seeing some of the many treasures of Sicily. Please thank the Principe for welcoming us to his house.
Yours sincerely,

Valeria Stanton, Bungay, Suffolk

Essences of the garden

Botanical name	Family
Acacia dealbata	leguminosæ
Acacia drepanolobium	leguminosæ
Acacia eucaliptoides	leguminosæ
Acacia farnesiana	leguminosæ
Acacia saligna	leguminosæ
Aeonium arboreum atropurpureum	crassulaceæ
Aeonium decorum coopery	crassulaceæ
Aeonium urbicum	crassulaceæ
Agave americana albicans	amaryllidaceæ
Agave americana marginata	amaryllidaceæ
Agave americana striata	amaryllidaceæ
Agave attenuata	amaryllidaceæ
Agave celsii	amaryllidaceæ
Agave colorata	amaryllidaceæ
Agave decipiens	amaryllidaceæ
Agave ferdinandi regii	amaryllidaceæ
Agave ferox	amaryllidaceæ
Agave filifera	amaryllidaceæ
Agave furcroydes	amaryllidaceæ
Agave lechuguilla	amaryllidaceæ
Agave lophanta poselgeri	amaryllidaceæ
Agave medio-picta alba	amaryllidaceæ
Agave medio-picta aurea	amaryllidaceæ
Agave noli tangere	amaryllidaceæ
Agave potatorum	amaryllidaceæ
Agave sisalana	amaryllidaceæ
Agave striata nana	amaryllidaceæ
Agave tetracantha	amaryllidaceæ

Albitia julibrissin	leguminosæ
Aloe arborescens	liliaceæ
Aloe aristata	liliaceæ
Aloe brevifolia	liliaceæ
Aloe ciliaris	liliaceæ
Aloe commixta	liliaceæ
Aloe comosa	liliaceæ
Aloe dichotoma	liliaceæ
Aloe ferox	liliaceæ
Aloe karlesbergensis	liliaceæ
Aloe macracantha	liliaceæ
Aloe marlothi	liliaceæ
Aloe microstigma	liliaceæ
Aloe mitriformis	liliaceæ
Aloe plicatilis	liliaceæ
Aloe pluridens	liliaceæ
Aloe saponaria	liliaceæ
Aloe striata	liliaceæ
Aloe variegata	liliaceæ
Aloe vera	liliaceæ
Aloe x humvir	liliaceæ
Annona cherimola	annonaceæ
Araucaria excelsa	araucariaceæ
Araucaria klinkii	araucariaceæ
Argyroderma villetii	aizoaceæ
Astrophytum miriostigma	cactaceæ
Astrophytum ornatum	cactaceæ
Bambusa	graminaceæ
Beaucarnea recurvata (nolina)	liliaceæ
Bouganvillæ albæ	nyctaginaceæ
Bouganvillæ buttiana	nyctaginaceæ
Bouganvillæ pretoriæ	nyctaginaceæ
Bouganvillæ sanderiana	nyctaginaceæ
Brachichiton	sterculiaceæ
Brahea armata	palmæ
Callistemon coccinea	myrtaceæ
Canna indica	cannaceæ

Carissa grandiflora	apocinaceæ
Caryota obtusa (ochlandra) fish tail palm	palmæ
Cassia excelsa	leguminosæ
Catecuja ipu	
Celtis australis (Bagolaro)	ulmaceæ
Cephalocereus polylophus	cactaceæ
Cercis siliquastrum (albero di Giuda)	leguminosæ
Cereus cesius monstruosus	cactaceæ
Cestrum nocturnum	solanaceæ
Chamerops humilis	palmæ
Chorisia speciosa	bombacaceæ
Citrus paradisii (pompelmo)	rutaceæ
Clivia miniata	amaryllidaceæ
Colletia armata	ramnaceæ
Colletia cruciata	ramnaceæ
Cotyledon macrantha virescens	crassulaceæ
Cotyledon orbilculata	crassulaceæ
Crassula argentea arborescens	crassulaceæ
Cycas revoluta	cycadaceæ
Cymbidium cambria	orchidaceæ
Cyperus papyrus	cyperaceæ
Dasylirion achrotiche	liliaceæ
Dasylirion glaucophillum	liliaceæ
Dasylirion longissimus	liliaceæ
Dasylirion serratifolium	liliaceæ
Dracæna draco	liliaceæ
Dracæna indivisa (cordyline australis)	liliaceæ
Echeveria agavoides	crassulaceæ
Echeveria pulvinata	crassulaceæ
Echeveria runyonii	crassulaceæ
Echeveria set-oliver	crassulaceæ
Echinocactus grusonii	cactaceæ
Echinopsis nigra	cactaceæ
Echium fastuosum	boraginaceæ
Encephalartos horridus	cycadaceæ
Eriobotrya japonica	rosaceæ
Erytrina caffra	leguminosæ

Erytrina cristagalli	leguminosæ
Eucaliptus camaldulensis	myrtaceæ
Eugenia Jambos	myrtaceæ
Euphorbia canariensis	euphorbiaceæ
Euphorbia grandealata	euphorbiaceæ
Euphorbia grandicornis	euphorbiaceæ
Euphorbia grandidens	euphorbiaceæ
Euphorbia lactea	euphorbiaceæ
Euphorbia pugniformis	euphorbiaceæ
Euphorbia pulcherrima	euphorbiaceæ
Euphorbia resineifera	euphorbiaceæ
Euphorbia virosa	euphorbiaceæ
Faucaria longifolia	aizoaceæ
Ficus benjamina	moraceæ
Ficus magnoloides	moraceæ
Ficus pumila (repens)	moraceæ
Freesia x hibrida	iridaceæ
Furcrea grigia	amaryllidaceæ
Furcrea selloa marginata	amaryllidaceæ
Gasteria lingua	liliaceæ
Gastrolea x beguinii	liliaceæ
Gazania splendens	compositæ
Grævillea robusta	protaceæ
Graptopetalum paraguayense	crassulaceæ
Gynerium sagittatum	graminaceæ
Hawortia tortuosa	liliaceæ
Hedera canariensis variegata	araliaceæ
Hedera canariensis	araliaceæ
Hedera helix	araliaceæ
Hibiscus rosa sin. ìCalifornia goldî	malvaceæ
Hibiscus rosa sinensis	malvaceæ
Hilocereus undatus	cactaceæ
Howeia forsetiana (kentia)	palmæ
Huernia zebrina	asclepiadaceæ
Iris germanica	iridaceæ
Iris pseudoaconis	iridaceæ
Kalanchoe marmorata	crassulaceæ

Kalanchoe tubiflora	crassulaceæ
Kleinia nerifolia	compositæ
Lampranthus emarginatus	aizoaceæ
Lampranthus tricolor	aizoaceæ
Lantana camara	verbenaceæ
Latania borbonica	palmæ
Laurus nobilis	lauraceæ
Lemaireocereus marginatus	cactaceæ
Lonicera caprifolium	caprifoliaceæ
Mammillaria candida	cactaceæ
Mammillaria celsiana	cactaceæ
Mammillaria elongata	cactaceæ
Mammillaria fragilis	cactaceæ
Mandevilla sanderi	apocynaceæ
Myrtillocactus cochal	cactaceæ
Myrtillocactus geometrzans	cactaceæ
Nerium oleander	apocynaceæ
Nopalea dejecta	cactaceæ
Olmo campestre	ulmaceæ
Opuntia cylindrica legnosa	cactaceæ
Opuntia cylindrica	cactaceæ
Opuntia dillenii	cactaceæ
Opuntia ficus-indica inermis	cactaceæ
Opuntia imbricata	cactaceæ
Opuntia leptocaulis	cactaceæ
Opuntia leucotricha	cactaceæ
Opuntia linguiformis	cactaceæ
Opuntia microdasys aurea	cactaceæ
Opuntia robusta	cactaceæ
Opuntia Santa Rita	cactaceæ
Opuntia tunicata argentea	cactaceæ
Opuntia vulgaris	cactaceæ
Orocereus celsianus	cactaceæ
Pachipodium geay	apocynaceæ
Pachipodium rosulatum	apocynaceæ
Parchinsonia aculeata	leguminosæ
Philodendron pertusum	araceæ

Philodendron selloum	araceæ
Phoenix canariensis	palmæ
Phoenix dactylifera	palmæ
Phoenix reclinata	palmæ
Pinus alepensis	pinaceæ
Pinus pinea	pinaceæ
Piperonia incanda	piperaceæ
Pittosporum tobira	pittosporaceæ
Platanus orientalis	platanaceæ
Plumbago alba	plumbacinaceæ
Plumbago capensis	plumbacinaceæ
Poinciana cæsalpinia	leguminosæ
Populus tremulus (Morocco's birch)	salicaceæ
Portulacaria afra	portulacaceæ
Punica melogranus	punicaceæ
Rosa alberique barbier	rosaceæ
Rosa andromeda	rosaceæ
Rosa appassionata	rosaceæ
Rosa banksia fortuniana	rosaceæ
Rosa cardinal de Richelieu	rosaceæ
Rosa casta diva	rosaceæ
Rosa castore	rosaceæ
Rosa clair matin	rosaceæ
Rosa longicuspis	rosaceæ
Rosa Marella Agnelli	rosaceæ
Rosa onda rosa	rosaceæ
Rosa penelope	rosaceæ
Rosa polluce	rosaceæ
Rosa Queen Elisabeth	rosaceæ
Rosa raubritter	rosaceæ
Rosa sea foam	rosaceæ
Rosa tesorino	rosaceæ
Rosmarinus officinalis	labiatæ
Sabal	palmæ
Salvia africana lutea	labiatæ
Salvia officinalis	labiatæ
Salvia sclarea	labiatæ

Schinus molle (false peppers)	anacardiaceæ
Sedum dendroideum	crassulaceæ
Sedum nussbaumerianus	crassulaceæ
Sedum rubropictum	crassulaceæ
Sempervivum tectorum calcareum	crassulaceæ
Senecio kleinia	compositæ
Senecium cineraria	compositæ
Setcrasea purpurea	commelinaceæ
Solandra major	solanaceæ
Solanum aviculare	solanaceæ
Solanum muricatum	solanaceæ
Stephanotis floribunda	asclepiadaceæ
Strelitzia augusta	musaceæ
Strelitzia reginæ	musaceæ
Tipuana tipu	leguminosæ
Trichocereus pasacana	cactaceæ
Trichocereus spachianus	cactaceæ
Viburnum (lantana) suspensum	caprifoliaceæ
Vinca major	apocynaceæ
Washingtonia filifera	palmæ
Washingtonia robusta	palmæ
Xanthorrea arborea	liliaceæ
Yucca aloifolia marginata	liliaceæ
Yucca aloifolia	liliaceæ
Yucca baccata	liliaceæ
Yucca elegantissima	liliaceæ
Yucca elephantipes	liliaceæ
Yucca filifera	liliaceæ
Yucca flaccida o gloriosa	liliaceæ
Yucca neo-mexicana	liliaceæ
Yucca rupicola	liliaceæ
Yucca speciosa	liliaceæ
Zantedeschia æthiopica (calla)	araceæ

Bibliography

"Ambiente 2000", December-January 1998-99.
"Amica", 1998.
"Belle Cose (Magazine for italian property)", 1998-99.
Cesare Brandi, *Sicilia mia*, Sellerio, Palermo 1989.
Case Country, in "Class", 1998.
Catalogo mostra storia del giardino, Orto botanico di Cagliari, 1998.
Chiara De Roo, in "Rivista Elle-Giardini", 1992.
"DOVE", De Agostini, 1994.
"Gardenia", Mondadori, Milan 1999.
"Giardinaggio", March 2002
"Giardini", Zanfi, 1998.
Giardini: Il nuovo Grand tour, Zanfi, 1999.
Giardiniere coraggiose, "Elle" Italian edition, 1997.
Guida Touring - I Giardini privati d'Italia, T.C.I., Milan 1999.
Verdant Harbour, *Patrick Bowe*, Country life, 1994.
Penelope Hobhouse, *Gardens of Italy*, Michel Beazley, 1997.
Robin Lane Fox, in "Financial Times-Gardening", October 1996.
Hugo Latimer, *The Mediterranean Gardener*, Royal Botanic Gardens, 1990.
Alessia Lefebure, in "Le Point", 1998.
Lorenza de' Medici, *The Renaissance of Italian Gardens*, Papillon, 1990.
News di Luise Allen, in "Rivista University of Oxford", 1998.
Paola Occhipinti, *Giardino Italia*, in "Verde oggi", 2000.
M.A. Paternò, *Luci ed ombre nei giardini siciliani*, Ist. Stat. d'arte CT, 1992.
"Qui Touring", Milan 1998.
Regione Siciliana, in "News", 1993.
Vittorio Sgarbi, *Il pensiero segreto*, Rizzoli, Milan 1990.
Gianni Pirrone, *Architettura dei Giardini di Sicilia*, Electa, Milan 1994.
Donatella Polizzi Piazza, *Etna Territorio*, 1993.
Raleigh Trevelyan, *The Companion Guide to Sicily*, St. Edmundsbury, 1996.

Index

Appendix

Silvana Editoriale

Via Margherita De Vizzi, 86
20092 Cinisello Balsamo, Milan
T 02 6172464 / 02 66046005
F 02 6172464
www.silvanaeditoriale.it

Printed and bound by
Arti Grafiche Amilcare Pizzi Spa
Cinisello Balsamo, Milan

May 2002